The First Rock 'n' Roll

BODYGUARD

Printed in the United Kingdom by Biddles Ltd, Surrey

Published by Sanctuary Publishing Limited, Sanctuary House, 45-53 Sinclair Road, London W14 0NS, United Kingdom

www.sanctuarypublishing.com

ISBN: 1-86074-328-5

The First Rock 'n' Roll
BODYGUARD
Alf Weaver with Robert Ashton

Contents

For Ella

This book is dedicated to Nordoff-Robbins Music Therapy

Introduction

For years now, I've been known in the British music industry as Mr Rock 'n' Roll Security. And for good reason. I've been the hired muscle on the shoulder of just about every pop and rock star. Going on tour? I'm the first call for every manager and record company. Get Alf on the blower, luv. Having a little party at the Met and want to keep the riff-raff out? Call Alf Weaver. Going to the BAFTAs? Going to the Brits? Do you think Alf will do it?

I carry the original gene for snuffing out trouble. I'm the blueprint for today's celebrity bodyguard. That's right. I pretty much invented the role. I was there first, looking after Otis Redding in Brixton, Sam And Dave, The Yardbirds. I was their first minder. The first rock 'n' roll bodyguard.

In the last four decades, I've worked all around the world. Any pop group went to Number One, I'd be their first-choice minder. I've fended off their fans, kept the unwanted attentions of the paparazzi at bay, swatted away nutters and kept groupies to manageable levels.

That meant I was there, on hand, at practically every epoch-making and icon-defining moment in pop- and rock-music history. I was on the roof of Apple's Savile Row offices when The Beatles played. I was in Hyde Park when the Stones played. I was in LA when The Doors played, strutting their stuff at the Whiskey A Go Go, slamming vodka sevens in the Rainbow room. I saw the real, raw, fast side of the early rock 'n' roll years, close up. I also witnessed, at first hand, the tantrums, fights, slaggings and personal scandals. Then I helped hide them from the headline-makers.

My company's Rolodex now reads like a rock superstar Who's Who – The Monkees, Frank Sinatra, Led Zeppelin, Dean Martin, Madonna, Cher, Rod Stewart, Tom Jones, Tony Bennett, David Bowie. I toured, ate and sometimes slept with these singers and groups, refereed their post-gig dust-ups and dealt with their drug dealers (I either paid them or bent them out of shape).

Now I've decided to put it all down on paper. Why not? I've hung up my dinner jacket and cummerbund and sold my company to the next generation of rock 'n' roll minders.

I also wanted to set the record straight about bodyguards. I know that most people see us as monkeys. Monkeys in monkey suits. Apes without a stick of wit. Yeah, there's some about, no doubt. But I'm not one of them. Tough, sure. Hard, yep. We've got to be. But there's much more to being a good minder than a good right fist. I'm living proof.

1 *Gimme Shelter*

I'm only five foot eight, but I've never been scared of anyone in my life. The Hell's Angel – all greasy, black leather and swastikas – had at least 15 pounds on me. I knew he was going to be trouble. But I could handle him.

It was a hot day. Humid, even. This was 5 July 1969, in the afternoon. Nearly half a million hippies, rock 'n' rollers, rockers, freaks, moonies, mods, druggies, Pearly Kings, Queens and the Hell's Angel and his gang of road rats were in London's Hyde Park. They were there to party with the best rock 'n' roll band in the world, The Rolling Stones. The Rolling Stones, ladies and gentleman. Brian Jones had been dead two days. It was a wild scene.

I'd just got back from the States, where I'd babysat one of The Monkees, and needed to earn a crust. The Stones gig was paying, and paying well. A fiver, I think. Remember, this was when half a nicker could buy you a good steak, a couple of glasses of Guinness and leave some change. My job was to run the stage. This meant kicking people off it.

The Rolling Stones were brought in by armoured car. The crowd parted. Those that didn't move quickly enough were belted out of the way by the outlaw bikers. The Stones wanted a bad-ass attitude, and the Hell's Angels were giving it to them. In spades. I spotted the swastika among the chromed German army helmets and wraparound shades. This Angel had no truck with the peace-and-love vibe. He pushed a teenage girl. Her boyfriend protested and he earned himself a beating – the Angel moved in quickly to stomp him with his engineer's boots. "Don't forget to bring flowers and love." Yeah, sure.

Backstage was a circus. Photographers, heavies, dealers, chicks. The Stones were holed up in a caravan and everyone wanted to get a piece of them. Was that Marianne Faithfull? There goes Ossie Clark, the designer. Paul McCartney. "Hello, Paul." Marsha Hunt. King Crimson's Robert

Fripp, one of the support acts. Alexis Korner's outfit, who'd just come offstage. It turned 5pm, 5.30pm, and suddenly the Stones were out. I spotted drummer Charlie Watts, steady and calm, in his own world. I'd known him for years, since driving for the Stones in their early days, and he was always a gent. "Go on, Charlie. Knock 'em dead." Charlie nodded. Charlie didn't talk much.

The group were breaking in new boy Mick Taylor. So this was Jones' replacement? Not a good choice. Taylor seemed to have less personality than his amp. Worse, he didn't walk or talk like a Stone. He just wasn't cool. Behind him, Keith Richards was giving pointers. "Fuck off, man," the surly guitarist advised anyone who strayed too close. "Fuck you." Standing near Richards, the focus of the Stones, Mick Jagger. In a white dress, it looked like. And is that make-up? Ponce, I thought.

The group hit the stage and the park exploded. "Cool it!" This was Jagger, camp but in control. "Cool it for a minute. I really would like to say something for Brian." I took up my usual position, stage right, and immediately sussed swastika and his mob. "Just cool it before we start." An evil sneer crept across the Angel's face, but a hush fell on the flower-powers. They stared up at Jagger in rapt silence. I was trying to earn myself a spot among the crush at the side of the stage, yards from Jagger. He started to read from a book:

> Peace, peace! He is not dead, he doth not sleep,
> He hath awakened from the dream of life.

Poetry. I found out later it was 'Adonais' by Shelley. Percy Bysshe. Never heard of him.

> 'Tis we who, lost in stormy visions, keep
> With phantoms an unprofitable strife,
> And in mad trance, strike with our spirit's knife
> Invulnerable nothings. – We decay
> Like corpses in a charnel; fear and grief
> Convulse us and consume us by day,
> And cold hopes swarm like worms within our living clay.

Christ. Jagger droned on, looking like a tart in that dress...

The One remains, the many change and pass;
Heaven's light forever shines, Earth's shadows fly;
Life, like a dome of many-coloured glass,
Stains the white radiance of Eternity,
Until Death tramples it to fragments. – Die,

...before stuttering to the end. Thank God for that.

If thou wouldst be that which thou dost seek!

Jagger nodded over to a couple of roadies at the front of the stage. They shook open some cardboard boxes and the sky was suddenly filled with thousands of white butterflies. Like unleashing Jones' soul, I guess. It was a bummer about Brian Jones. He was younger than me. Drowned by a couple of drunk labourers. That was the story, anyway. But you got used to people dying in this business.

Then Richards began chopping out chords. 'I'm Yours, She's Mine'. This was more like it. The band was a bit ragged, but the place began to rock. 'Jumpin' Jack Flash', 'Mercy Mercy', 'Down Home Girl', 'Lovin' Cup'. 'Honky Tonk Women', one of my favourites. Yeah, that was more like it. Better than poetry. 'Midnight Rambler'. '(I Can't Get No) Satisfaction'. "We can get ourselves satisfaction. You can get yourselves some satisfaction. We could all get ourselves some satisfaction." Now they were moving and onto 'Street Fighting Man'.

By the time Jagger began strutting to 'Sympathy For The Devil', we'd been throwing fans back into the crowd all day long, but it was good-natured stuff. Then I caught sight of the Hell's Angel again. His gang of stormtroopers had been drinking and meting out its own brand of violence to any incense-burning hippies that wandered into their orbit. This was insane brutality. They smashed deck-chairs – they battered one couple who wouldn't give theirs up – and used them to light a fire. One kid, not even 18, had his face carved up when one self-styled wild child crushed a full beer can into it. His crime? Having a good time. I'd been watching those fucks and it was pathetic.

Now one young chick, all flower-power and yellow buttercups, danced near the outlaw biker. He gave her a slap and she spun around, surprised. I didn't dig that, as Jagger might have said. The Angel laughed, revealing blackened teeth rotted by speed. The girl began to cry. I'd had enough. I jumped down from the stage and pushed out towards the greaser. He saw me coming, but not the punch. My thing is, hit first. I caught him with a left jab and followed up – hard – with a swift right hook. *Crack.* That busted his nose up and took him down. He got back on his knees. Blood was trickling down his nose. He wiped it away with the back of his hand and looked up. I was waiting. I'd hurt him, but not enough. He moved back onto his heels and crouched. We stared at each other for what seemed like hours. I could see his black, dilated eyes. They were dead, just like a shark I'd seen on TV. Nothing much going on behind them. He was going to rush me. I knew that. It was just a matter of when. He was still on his haunches, blood dripping down onto his oil-stained Levis.

Suddenly, he was up. I knew he'd have to make a move – his gang were watching. I hoped they'd stay out of it. We were a couple of yards apart, too far to control him. I wasn't going to wait for him to make the move. I stepped forward to narrow the distance, moved left and shot out a quick right to his jaw. I heard it pop. He stumbled forward but managed to stay upright. He looked around, searching out his mates. I looked, too. The Hell's Angels glared over but didn't move an inch. Swastika was on his own. This time, he stood his ground. As well as his extra weight, he was at least six-one, his sunglasses were busted up and he was leaking blood from his crooked nose. He swung. A real haymaker. He should have posted it. It would have arrived quicker.

Missed.

We were close now, and I moved in to deliver some body shots. *Duh, duh, duh.* It was all over for him. I felt his body sag and he dropped.

Someone passed me some draw. The bikers were finished that afternoon, but a few months later a Californian chapter of the Hell's Angels killed Meredith Hunter at the Altamont Speedway. They stabbed him to death as Jagger sang 'Sympathy For The Devil'. I turned back towards the stage, where Jagger and Richards were wrapping things up. They can't have imagined what they'd face before the year was out. "Hope ya had a good time. We gotta go. We gotta. Oh, baby, what's my name? Oh yeah…" I watched the show for a few moments from the crowd. It was getting late. It felt like the end of the '60s. I was tired.

2 Street Fighting Years

He was a boxer, Ronnie Bradstreet. He was also my best friend. Ronnie and I thought we owned those streets in our little neighbourhood. We knew every alley in Camden Town. Looking back to those old days, it seemed as though colour hadn't been invented and that England was black and white. Businessmen wore charcoal pinstripe suits and bowler hats, the smoke pouring out of the chimneys on our street was black, and if we were lucky enough to spot a car that day I'd have laid you odds of two to one on that it would be black.

Of course, it wasn't just black and white. There were other colours. Grey was a favourite – grey underpants, grey sheets, grey rain, grey days. That's what I remember about those early years. But then, I was born into the Depression, on the last day of March 1935, so I had it coming.

I was born Alfred Charles, after my old man, right next to the railway track that threads through north London and crosses Hawley Road, around by number 27. That's where I lived for the first few years of my life. It was one of those big, tall Victorian terraces split into a warren of flats. Grey brick, slate roof. Ratty curtains and yellowing photos on the wall. We had a small kitchen and a few rooms, sharing the bathroom with a couple of other families. That's how it was, then. We'd stay a few months, maybe even years in a good place, before quitting, usually one step ahead of the landlord. But we would only move one or two streets away. I still remember the addresses, and they're all within a couple of square miles, around Camden and Kentish Town.

By the time I'd learned my first swear words, the Germans were bombing London. I was evacuated, along with the rest of the kids in my neighbourhood. Firstly, I was packed off to a family in Kettering, but it didn't work out. I was made to sleep in the bath, and that didn't impress my mother, who came down to fetch me back. The railway yards were the main target of the bombers, but hundreds of houses were destroyed, and early in the war Camden underground station was bombed, killing four people. When the sirens sounded, we'd run the few hundred yards along Camden High Street and down into the tube. It was always dark going down those steps into the passages and platforms below the street. And the smell! That's what I remember most about hiding down in those tunnels while bombs flattened our houses above. It's difficult to describe the smell of hundreds of bodies crammed together on narrow platforms, half a century on. It was musty. There was sweat, and there was also fear. The babies always seemed to be crying.

By this time, I was being schooled by the Dominican Brothers at St Dominic's Roman Catholic School, a red-brick pile on Southampton Road. It was only a short walk up Maldon Road from where we were then living, at the top of a two-storey house at 236 Grafton Road. It seemed like we couldn't escape the railway track. It ran right behind the house. I didn't stay long because the Blitz soon kicked in big-time and my older brother, Dennis, and I were packed off to stay with a couple, the Knowles, in Cornwall. With London hundreds of miles away, the war was soon forgotten. This was a happy experiment. There was a farm next door to the house we stayed at, and Dennis, who was then nine, worked the land while I played with some of the animals. Many years later, we dropped in on Mr Knowles and he showed us up to our old bedroom, where nothing – not even the flock wallpaper – had been changed. I opened a drawer and there were our tiny old wool sweaters, neatly folded, just as we'd left them.

One of the priests from St Dominic's Priory, right next door to our school, came down to keep us up with our schooling. "Come on, lads. We've work to be done." But mostly, he just scared the bejesus out of the villagers. He strode down the street in his long, flowing black robes and boots and people would run and hide. They'd seen nothing like him.

After two years, we were back in north London, at a new address, on Truro Street, in Kentish Town. The place was almost unrecognisable. Whole streets had disappeared and the families with them.

The family had grown while I'd been away. I had a little sister, Ann. The first time I saw her, she was nearly two. I'd been too young to get into any jams in Cornwall, but back in the Smoke there was plenty to occupy a seven-year-old boy.

The railway sheds at the top of the road were used to store coal for the steam trains. We never had enough money to keep our fires going, so

Alf (far left) with brother Dennis, sister Ann and mother Elizabeth

Alf's father, Charlie (far left), at a pub in Camden Town

Aunt Theresa (middle)

Dennis and I would break in to thieve sacks of the stuff. Those winters were always freezing, when I was a kid. I'd go to bed in the same clothes I wore during the day.

I was back at St Dominic's for just over a year when the V2 doodlebugs began raining on London. This time it was me and Ann who got evacuated, to stay with a coal-miner and his family in Tonypandy, South Wales. There was no shortage of coal now, and sometimes he'd take me down into the shafts to watch the miners work the seams. Friday nights were special. The coal-miner's wife worked in a chippy, and we'd run around to grab a salty bag of fish and chips soaked in vinegar. A real treat.

With the war over, we got back to London. It took me a few months to shake off a Welsh accent I'd picked up. My mother did her best, but food rationing was still in force after the war and trying to make a meat-and-two-veg meal was never an option. Food was boiled, broiled or burnt. Sometimes all three. And it smelled. Usually of cabbage, which got right into the walls and clothes. You could never escape it.

But there was always something going on outside school. We'd go nicking from shops. "Hey, come back you little bastard!" We'd scrump apples, pick over the debris in bombed-out houses, maybe even sell scrap or firewood for a tanner. There used to be a sweet shop on Chalk Farm Road whose owner had a fiddle going with rationing coupons. And then we moved again. This time it was into the house next door.

My old man, Charlie, hadn't been around much. He'd been in the Royal Artillery in the war, stationed in India, and didn't seem in a hurry to get back. When he did, he took a job as a sheet-metal worker near Warren Street. My mother had brought us up, and my father didn't get involved too much. We weren't close. He got into the drink and often spent his evenings and most weekends with a pint of ale in his hand at the local boozer, the Queen's Head.

I don't know if this caused problems with my parents, but the strain was beginning to tell on my mother, and she was often ill. When I was twelve, she died. What a nightmare. She came from a family of a dozen brothers and sisters, and one of them, Aunt Theresa, came to keep us on the straight and narrow. I guess that, being older, Dennis may have been too much of a handful, and he started to get into scrapes with the law. However, Theresa kept me off the streets and out of trouble when we moved to 167 Arlington Road, right next door to the Shrine Of Our Lady of Hal Catholic Church. We had all come up in the faith, and she encouraged me to become an altar boy at the small Belgian church. Not that this was an easy option; I'd wake up, go in at 8.30am, do four masses on Sunday morning and Benediction in the afternoon.

I also found myself another religion: I was starting to get into football. The nearest club to our house was Arsenal, the Gunners, in Highbury, and they were riding high. My dad was also a die-hard fan. With manager George Allison, they'd won the 1936 FA Cup against Sheffield United and were league champions, again, in the 1937-38 season. The ground was commandeered by the army during the war, but when the team moved back to Highbury, my old man got us tickets for one of the first post-war games. We'd stand on the North Bank, a massive stack of terraces at one end of the ground for the home fans. "Arsenal, Arsenal, Arsenal." Kids my age would be passed down over the heads of the crowd so we could watch the game from the front, just yards from the pitch. This was the time when the crowds would regularly be over 60,000 and legendary players like the Compton brothers, Leslie and Denis, Swindin and Mercer, were at the height of their powers. "Arsenal, Arsenal, Arsenal." I could hear every grunt and thud of the lead-heavy leather. From my first visit to Highbury, I fell in love with the team, and nearly 60 years later I still watch every home game yards from where I stood as a kid.

Arsenal also meant my father and I found a connection. I would meet him from work on Saturday lunchtime and join the crowds teeming out of the pubs to walk to the ground. The atmosphere was electric. I loved everything about match day: the smells of the hot-dog stands, the cries of the programme-sellers, the banter, the arguments over the team, the songs. And then there was the anticipation of the game itself, which multiplied ten-fold on derby days against other London teams, like arch-rivals Tottenham Hotspur. I could hardly wait for the whistle to blow at three o'clock, and my stomach twisted into anxious knots.

Even the ground, with its beautiful art deco entrance and cool marble halls, seemed special. I was so much in love with the place I often used to tramp the four or five miles from Arlington Street to Highbury to stand outside the ground and listen to the crowd. I could tell if Compton was spinning his magic, or if Lewis had hit a dry spell, just from the cheers, groans or nervy silence. I also saw Leslie Compton make his England debut against France at Highbury. He was well into his 30s then, and had a great

Camden Town's Seafarers team. (Alf back row, fifth from left)

team around him – Billy Wright, Stan Matthews, Tommy Lawton, Tom Finney. England won two-nil.

With Tom Whittaker in charge in the dressing room, Arsenal won the 1947-48 championship by seven points. Later, I got tickets for the 1950 FA Cup final, when Arsenal beat Liverpool two-nil, and have seen every single final played at Wembley since, regardless of whether the Gunners were playing.

I was also playing football. I'd kick a ball around in the street, and I spent long hours bashing one against the back wall. *Dud-ah, dud-ah, dud-ah*. I'd thud it all afternoon to practise with both feet and the noise would drive my aunt mad. I was picked to either play left back or left wing half. I wasn't a bad dribbler. I'd play for the school on Saturday before racing down to Highbury to watch Arsenal, and for my youth club – the Seafarers, on Camden Street – on Sunday. Sometimes as many as 500 people would turn out for our games in Regent's Park or Primrose Hill, especially if we were playing the local mob from a rival youth club on Medburn Street, in Somerstown. We made it to the FA Youth Club championship one year, but Crown and Manor put us out before we got near the final.

In early May 1953, the Seafarers held a raffle. I won. Two tickets to watch Bolton versus Blackpool. The Matthews final. The legendary winger Stanley Matthews had been transferred to Blackpool a few years before and dominated the game. Bolton went one-nil up. They might have won, but they lost a player and, with no substitutes, had to play the remainder of the game with ten men. Blackpool took over. Two goals from Mortensen. Then Matthews, down the right wing on a dribble. He went left, swerved right, centred for Perry. Thud. Goal. That was something.

I was a dunce at school. I couldn't be bothered. I hated all the lessons. Just stared out of the window. If you didn't know the answers, you held your hand out and – *whack!* – got caned. I got caned a lot. My only interest was football, but I was getting interested in girls. There was Sheila, on Eversholt Street, and a girl called Jean. She lived near a mate of mine, Terry Underwood, on Jeffrey's Street.

I bunked off some school with Terry and Ronnie Bradstreet. We'd sneak into the back of the local picture house to catch a glimpse of Humphrey Bogart or catch a variety show at the Bedford Music Hall. This was like a palace – heavy Victorian reds, mosaic floor, thick velvet seats and gilded ceiling. Max Miller played there once. Two and a kick a show. Occasionally we'd get caught, and that meant a visit to the headmaster, Mr Norton. "Six of the best, boy." *Whacky-whack!* He was always dishing it out. But it only stung for a couple of hours. Next day, we'd be back hanging out around Camden Parkway or having a quick puff in St Martin's Fields.

We also got into fights. St Dominic's was a rough old place, and there were scraps every day. And when we weren't fighting each other, a gang of us would walk a mile down the road to take on a school on Royal College Street. There was always somebody around who wanted a knuckle. These were our Camden Town street-fighting years. Fortunately, one of the best fighters was Ronnie.

We figured we would come out on top of a lot more scraps if we knew a little something about boxing. They had some old gloves at the Seafarers and a ring set up. I liked the training. It was hard, but it kept us in shape. Former middleweight contender Charlie Webster worked at the Seafarers and helped train us. I learned to punch the bag and skip rope on Camden Street. Fighters now have one punch; Charlie taught me all the combinations – left jab, straight right, jab, jab, jab. *Bam. Bam. Bam.* When you're in a clinch, you give them one in the side, then go for the body. You work up and down. I had all the tricks down. Then we'd go for five- and ten-mile runs up near Hampstead. I could handle myself. And I got better in school scraps. One time, some kids thought they'd work me over. I don't remember what it was about. Probably nothing. I picked out the biggest. He was heavily built. Jab, *bam.* I had him stumbling and smacked him about with a few more jabs. He was getting cut up pretty bad and swinging wildly. Then I dropped him with one punch, right on the chin. I knew where to hit and when. The others just melted away, and that was a lesson learned: always go for the biggest bastard. If you do him, you won't have trouble again. No one picked on me or my mates again.

I used to box at school in the day and at the Seafarers at night. We moved again – no surprise there – to a grim council flat at 31 Rugemere House, Ferdinand Street, off the Chalk Farm Road. The good news was that Ronnie lived right across the street. After school, I'd call around for him and we'd hit the Seafarers.

We were both lightweights and used to spar together. When the fair came to town, we used to fight in the spit-and-sawdust boxing booth. To win a prize – some crap – you only had to last three rounds, which we mostly did. I was getting good. I must have had about 50 fights. I won a couple of London schoolboys' titles.

I remember boxing one guy up in Manor Park. This was the final of the National Federation of Boys' Clubs in 1951. I was 16. A photographer came to the Seafarers to take a picture for the local rag, *The Evening Star.* My opponent saw it. "This you?"

"Yeah. What about it?"

He thought I was a celebrated prize-fighter and was already scared when he stepped into the ring. I only hit him a couple of times before he went down. The fight was stopped. England had a new teenage champ. "Alf Weaver, winner." That sounded pretty good.

Another time, I had a fight in a gym above a pub. It was a tough brawl. That's why I probably remember it. Full house, but dancing in my corner, I couldn't make out the crowd, only the glow from their cigarettes. I could hear them, though. What a racket! Charlie was in my corner and kept shouting advice, but I didn't hear a word. Then the referee called us into the centre of the ring, we tapped gloves and then, *whoosh!* The minutes went like seconds. It was a blaze of jabs, punches and uppercuts. I slid in under a couple of useful shots before smashing in a couple to his body. I heard him grunt and knew I'd hurt him. I bulled him onto the ropes and tried to smash him to the canvas, but he was too good for that. He soaked up the punishment before slipping me a feint and stepping in to catch me with one, two, three cuts at my gut. *Ding, ding.* The bell.

Charlie washed the grease and sweat from my eyes and checked my gloves. I was already panting heavily. *Ding.* Second round.

We'd both got our game going now. Air rushed into my lungs and came out as a short grunt with every punch I threw. *Hoo. Hoo.* I was bobbing and weaving, flicking out my left. I've always had a good left hand. I wasn't getting hit. Then he feinted, stepped back and took up a southpaw stance. This momentarily shook me, and in that second he lashed out a powerful right, which stunned me and sent me reeling. I was now also fighting my legs to stay upright as he rushed me across the ring. He tried another big haymaker, but I somehow managed to block it and dodged to counter with my reliable left jab. I connected, and that started to sting him; he eased back. Suddenly, I saw an opening when he moved back to a conventional stance and dropped his guard. *Wham!* Bullseye. One shot was all it took. Right on the button, at the bottom of his jaw. He crumpled. I saw Charlie first, punching the air. The referee raised my right hand, and then I heard the crowd. I could now see them. I saw the kids from my school class. And the girls. Who'd have thought they would be interested in seeing us get beat up? But they were cheering, too. I liked that. I felt my nose. It was broken, but that was the first and last boxing injury I got.

Ronnie wasn't as lucky. He was the better boxer. We talked and breathed the game together. My hero was Joe Louis, the Brown Bomber. He had the shortest knock-out punch. Six inches, lights out. Ronnie soon got a lot of guys telling him to turn pro. He was a natural talent and was getting there, moving up his division. Then he had one hard fight too many and, although he won, he took a bad beating.

His manager was a bum. That's the thing with boxing. Managers seem to be the ones who make all the money, not the fighters. This manager wanted to put Ronnie in another fight the next week. "It'll be

The Seafarers' boxing team (Alf third from left, front row)

The Camden boxers, including Terry Underwood, Harry Champion and Alf

Alf the young pugilist in Camden Town

Alf in an early bout

easy. Trust me. This guy's a pushover." Easy for him. He wasn't in the ring. Ronnie didn't want the fight. He told me, "It's too early. I don't feel right." He should have rested up, but his manager kept on at him and eventually Ronnie took it. It was at the baths on the Prince Of Wales Road in Kentish Town, half a nicker at the door, and it was another tough match. I could see Ronnie wasn't punching like normal and he was getting hit. Boxing's a hard game, but as I watched my stomach was cramping up. I knew Ronnie was getting hurt in there. He lost. Ronnie walked out of the ring but collapsed hours later and was rushed to hospital with a brain haemorrhage. He didn't regain consciousness again and died the following day. I was angry and felt sick. He was my best friend. I lost my taste for boxing, but I kept hold of the gloves. Just in case.

School couldn't finish early enough. I was 14 when I left. What did I know? No maths, my spelling was rubbish, and nothing about world affairs. I wasn't going to make it as a lawyer. But Goddard & Phillips, a painting and decorating firm up in Kentish Town, was hiring. What a lark! Now I'll never hire a painter, after working that business. In the '50s, only wealthy Londoners could afford not to decorate their own homes, so we were always sent out to fancy neighbourhoods like Hampstead or Holland Park, where the big old houses had so much white stucco they looked like wedding cakes. The idea was to look like you were working but keep the pace slow and steady. I started as an apprentice, so my job was the least taxing – I opened the paint tins and cut the wallpaper. Later, I did undercoats. But no one ever broke sweat. I'd catch the underground to arrive early, but then it was a tea break every half hour, ten minutes for a fag break, another break to take a leak, then lunch (usually a sandwich made from anything we could find in the kitchen), more tea, more cigarettes, piss, tea, fag, 5pm. "OK, boys. That's it. See you tomorrow." We could spin a one-week job into a month.

There were plenty of other jobs, too. My aunt's family worked at a place down on St Pancras Way, near King's Cross. An engineering factory called White's. It was piecework, and I did a few shifts lifting bales of wire. That was a few extra coppers. It also kept me fit and strong. Good training. Maybe I was getting bored, but when the army got me in 1953, I wasn't too upset. Unless you wore bottle-bottom glasses or had a gammy leg, National Service was something everyone did when they turned 18. I was assigned to the First Battalion Rifle Brigade, a London mob. This was going to be like the Seafarers. Or so I thought.

What followed was ten weeks of basic training in Winchester. Basic boring, more like. It was drill, potato peeling, kit and shoe polishing. I spent long hours hunched up over my bunk working up phlegm. Spit and rub. Spit and rub. I hated drill and guard duties, but then I got a tip about how to avoid them: the army went soft on members of sports teams. I hadn't boxed since Ronnie's death and wasn't keen to pick up the gloves again, but fighting got me assigned to the officers' mess as a waiter. Cushy. Every time I was up for guard duty, Major Wilson, who was in charge of the boxing team, told the company sergeant I was too busy. I was soon battalion champion, and the major didn't want to tire his best fighter. We had shiny boots but couldn't shoot a barn door by the time we were sent on to Bulford in Wiltshire to complete battle training and wait for our orders.

The Korean War was raging. We'd all heard about the last stand of the Glorious Gloucesters. Fifty-nine lives lost, nearly 600 men captured. Word got out that we should prepare to embark for Seoul and we were

Alf's uncle, who was a bare-knuckle fighter

issued our winter kit. Suddenly spit and rub didn't look too onerous. However, before the government risked another military disaster by sending a bunch of green squaddies to fight, the war was over. We waited it out for a new posting. I could see my reflection in my boots by the time the orders came through. This time it was Kenya, to quell the Mau Mau Insurrection. No problem.

In the weeks before we were posted, some of the boys spread stories about the Mau Maus' supposed initiation ceremonies. They sounded hardcore: hack someone to death, then drink their blood. Despite this, I was more excited – this was my first taste of foreign travel – than scared when we pitched up in Liverpool to board the troopship *HMS Georgic*. It was a slow, leisurely voyage. We rigged up a boxing ring on the ship's deck and fought numerous bouts under the blazing sun every day of the four-week trip.

I also made it into the battalion football team. We sailed through the Suez Canal and on to Kenya, where we docked at Mombasa. The footballers – and only the players – were allowed to disembark to play a game against a team of locals from the town. The Africans didn't wear boots, but their feet were as hard as iron when they tackled. My shins could vouch for that! And they ran rings around us on the dry, rutted pitch. They had a right winger. Nippy fella. Very fast. This was who I was supposed to mark. "Go on, Alf, get stuck in there." I couldn't get near him. Two-one, we lost, and we were lucky with that.

Our company was stationed near the Aberdare Forest. We caught the train in country to Nairobi and then north to Fort Hall and on to Nanyuki. We moved around as we chased the Mau Maus – Nyeri, Nakuru, Gilgil, Naivasha. The uprising was at its height, with European settlers being murdered almost weekly. The terrorists demanded fierce loyalty from villagers through intimidation and extreme violence. Killings – often of children – were commonplace. Our job was to move them out of the villages and forests where they hid and up into the mountains. Our camps were always under canvas, and Major Wilson would only select a base if there was a nearby patch of flat land to play football on.

Kenya was full of animals. I'd never seen as many birds, every kind of bird. Giraffes, monkeys and zebras, which always got run over by our trucks. Sometimes on patrol, out on the plains, we'd get chased by buffalo.

The Seafarers Club drinking in Belgium. (Alf far right)

Fierce beasts. One time, we also got caught by a herd of elephants. It was like a block of flats coming towards us. Someone shouted for us to dive right. We all leapt out of our skins and 50 tons ran past us, the ground shaking beneath us.

I was now head of the officers' mess. Mess life was different from training camp – I didn't have to make my bed or square anything up. Spit and rub. Spit and rub. Forget about it. And potato peeling? Not me. There was no kit inspection, officers spared me guard duty and on pay day, when the rest of the company formed an orderly queue, I'd walk right to the front to pick up my monthly wages. The lads would wolf-whistle as I walked the line. I loved it in the mess. It was a different life, and all down to the boxing.

I remember one fight out in Uganda, during a spot of R&R. I was boxing for the British army against the Ugandan Amateur Boxing Association in Kampala. At the time, they were training for the Olympics. I was number one on the team but wasn't 100 per cent and swapped with my pal, who fought their top man. Not that their number two was a pushover. Far from it. We were in the open, outside, and it was hot. Very hot.

Alf (left) at Winchester barracks in the army

He was up and off straight from the bell. We went at it like crazy, and he was having some. He knocked me down halfway through the first round. I was lucky to get up, but got on my knee. I settled for a moment and looked over at my pals from the company. They weren't smiling. I knew I had to win this. I got knocked down again. I saw stars and the first round wasn't even over. Army pride was at stake and I was almost spent, dog tired. I waited for the count to reach eight before getting up. My legs had gone already, and I knew the next two rounds were going to be hell. *Ding-a-ling*. The bell. That bell saved me. In the second round, he came again, too fast and slightly off balance. That was my opening. *Wham!* My left jab connected. That hurt him, and I jabbed again. *Wham!* I didn't throw a right for the rest of the match. *Wham! Wham! Wham!* I got the result. The guy came over to me: "What happened to your right hand? I was waiting for it." He'd never been hit by so many lefts.

The difficulty was knowing who was Mau Mau. Someone could be a houseboy by day and turn freedom-fighter at night. That's when evil stalked, when the murders happened. Trying to fight terrorists was like hunting needles in a very big haystack. We'd run ambushes and patrols for a month or so, a few pints in the NAAFI, back on patrol, a week's R&R in Mombasa and back again. When we ran over the Mau Mau camps, we'd always find bits of men cut to pieces – heads, part of an arm lying around. The places used to stink, but strangely I wasn't affected. I suppose I was young. If you see an arm, it's just an arm. The African police would check out the villagers to see if any Mau Mau were still around. Usually they were long gone.

However, we had a few contacts. I remember one ambush. We used to lie in wait next to the paths twisting through the forests. I'd sit in my tin hat, completely camouflaged and completely still. Very still, for hours and hours in the thick bamboo. Any sound – a bird, a branch breaking – was like an explosion. That first hour, I'd think about how we'd handle the Mau Mau if they came. How many would there be? They were small, wiry and tough as hell. What if they were heavily armed? What would happen if I was taken prisoner? That one made me sweat. Then I'd start dreaming, thinking about my family, boxing, home, football – "Arsenal, Arsenal, Arsenal" – life after the army, anything. Sometimes I'd drift off for a few minutes.

This night, we found a track which the Mau Mau were using to shift supplies. It was cold, wet and boring. It was almost a full moon, a good night for the Mau Mau to move. A good night to attack them.

The night was turning to dawn when a handful of terrorists came down the trail. I heard their machetes first. They were hacking back branches and, although they were whispering, we could hear them from hundreds of yards away. Every time they hacked at a branch, it sounded like thunder, like the loudest thing I'd heard in my life, and it seemed to take them hours to move a few yards. I wasn't scared – I'd trained for this – but I was concentrating hard, my heart pounding in my chest and breathing fast. I was more focused than I'd ever been, even in a fight.

We listened, and they came closer. Closer. Closer. Slowly. I could hear the whispering getting louder, even make out different voices now. Not yet. Wait. And then one started to laugh about something. They all stopped and had a good laugh now. There was a comedian out there. Mau Mau jokes.

Then it suddenly struck me that, within seconds, the joker would be dead. I might even kill him. Strange, that. You always try and block out things like that. I didn't want to think about this Mau Mau having a wife, maybe even a few kids. Then they started up again. *Come on!* I was sweating, breathing, trying not to make a sound. They passed me and I waited for a signal. The drill was always the same, at least it was supposed to be: hold anyone up and challenge them. If they were Mau Mau... Suddenly the whole forest started blazing. Fuck! Someone hadn't waited for the challenge. There was the *crack! crack! crack!* of the FM rifle, rounds thudding into bark. I stood and let rip with my gun in the direction of the trail. Someone had a Bren gun, and I could hear them putting out at least half a magazine of .303s. *Rat-a-tat-tat.* That was some firefight. I don't know how many rounds the Mau Mau got off, but they were dead within seconds. The joker, too.

Back at company HQ, Captain Somerset had been impressed by an Italian POW's account of his attempt on Mount Kenya. The POW had been held in a prison camp in the shadow of the mountain and spent any spare moment fashioning equipment to help him climb it after the war. Somerset went for it. Why not follow the POW's journey? He wanted seven other men for a team and I was in the frame.

Fifth platoon, B company

Clowning around in the army

Hunting the Mau Mau in Kenya, 1955

From my bunk, I had regularly watched the weather sweep off the mountain, changing dramatically from hour to hour. Bathed in sunlight, the snowy peak looked like a beautiful, peaceful place. An hour later, obscured by thick cloud and swirling snow, I wouldn't send my worst enemy up there. Now we were going to make an attempt on the 14,000-foot peak. I'd never climbed anything higher than a tree before. None of us had. We raided stores to kit ourselves out in any winter gear we could find. There wasn't any – this was Africa – so we just took two of everything and hoped for the best. Some guys in the battalion fashioned some home-made crampons to tackle the ice fields near the summit, but none of us knew what we were letting ourselves in for.

Somerset roped us together and up we went. Up, up, up. The first couple of days, in the foothills, was a breeze. Gentle slopes, the sun on our backs. No Mau Mau up there. Easy. But when we reached the snowline, I was feeling the pace. We climbed without oxygen and...the higher we got...the more stops...we made...to catch...our breath. It was like walking on treacle, when we hit a boulder field. One step forward, slip and slide back. With the thin air and a full pack, that was tiring. Very tiring.

But we were lucky with the weather. It blew up rough one day and we walked around in circles for hours before deciding to sit it out, huddled together in a snow storm, trying to pitch tents in a gale, freezing, fingers numb with cold and just hoping it would end soon. But we didn't lose anyone. Somerset was proud of that.

And what a view when we made the summit! It was cold, but not that cold, and it was clear. We could see for miles – our camp, the football pitch nearby, the forest beyond. It felt like I was looking down on the whole of Africa. We sat on the peak for hours, tossing rocks down the slopes and toasting ourselves with tea from a British-army-issue tin cup. I felt like I'd done something special. Only a few months before, I'd never stepped outside of England. Now I was sitting on top of the world. OK, Mount Kenya.

In 1955, my National Service ended. Before I was demobbed, the CO, Colonel Boden, asked me to sign on for a couple of years. The next posting was Malaya. I didn't fancy that. Because of my experience in the officers' mess, Boden gave me a letter of introduction to work at his club in London. It was White's. Churchill was a member. So was Lord

Mountbatten. I was a waiter earning three quid – a carpet – every week. For the next eight months, I served lunches and dinners and a bunch of politicians and bankers got fat.

3 On The Knocker

I was 20 in London in the mid '50s. A good time. Money was still tight, but not like before I went into the army. I was back with the Seafarers and out with Terry Underwood. We hit the West End at weekends to check out the American stars playing the Palladium, Val Parnell's place. Dean Martin and Jerry Lewis. Johnny Ray – 'Glad Rag Doll', 'Little White Cloud'. Frankie Laine, Al Martino, Danny Kaye. On Sundays we'd catch The Ted Heath Band – 'Night Train', *whoo-whoo* – at the Pal. Maybe go down the Trocadero. We also checked out the girls. I was in shape from the boxing and football. The army had also taught me to dress smart – black tie, white shirt. Nice shoes. Polished, of course. I had some success with the ladies in the back row of the ABC. Chips Rafferty in *King Of The Coral Sea*, or *Contraband Spain*. Then maybe grab a bag of chips and a light ale before last orders.

White's was good, but it wasn't Kenya. I was looking for more action than watching Sir This or Lord That stuffing his face. They were a snotty bunch, always bossing us about and never a please or thank you. Then my brother turned up. I told him how much I was pulling down at the St James club. "You're mad. I can get you that in a day." Dennis was on the knocker. I was sold.

There were four or five other fellas in our knocking gang. Dennis ran it. In the evenings we'd load up a van at a firm called Presant & Fisher, down the back of King's Cross. Blankets, rugs, sheets, soap, pegs, you name it. Any crap that most people didn't need but thought they wanted after they'd been sold on ten minutes of patter. Around six the next morning, we'd head off for Manchester, Nottingham, Birmingham, Leeds, Oxford, Hull even, anywhere we hadn't been for a few weeks, and sell. We'd work the streets, where the best customers – and payers – lived, then move onto the council estates or the high-rises. I had the sales rap off pat. I had it down. *Tap tap tap.* "Come on, darling. Look at that." I've pulled out a blanket. "Pure new wool." It was coarse as fuck and made of something like horsehair, but what the heck. "Come on, what do you say? Three shillings and it's yours." *Tap tap*. "Hello. Short of nylons?" *Tap tap*. "Look at this. You can feel it's top-quality gear." We'd get rid of the stuff and then a few days later a credit company would turn up to collect, a few bob a week. The credit company would pay Fisher's and we'd pick up commission on what we sold. It was good money.

One of our best earners was paraffin heaters. We sold hundreds of these little burners to Jamaican immigrants holed up in freezing tenements. They were only supposed to be lit for a few hours, but they had them fired up all day long and every now and again they'd overheat and burn a place down.

Tap tap tap. If Dennis saw I was struggling with a sale, he'd come over and do his spiel: "This is your genuine Irish linen. You're saving money in the long run, luv. Come on, we're practically giving this little lot away." *Tap tap tap*. Sometimes I'd get invited in for a lot more than a cup of tea. A lot of these birds were married, some had kids, and they were all bored. It was a perk of the job. And we were all at it.

One time, I was getting along pretty good with a girl in York. Nice girl. Brunette, I think, with all the right curves in all the right places. I'd been trying to sell her some rugs. "Genuine wool, that is. You won't find anything cheaper." She was more interested in the sheets I was holding, or getting between them. I was in and out of the bedroom in less than an hour, just as her husband rolled up from work. A real dope. I wasn't surprised she was looking for a bit of action on the side. He didn't look happy, but what was he going to do? Besides, he couldn't be certain what had been going on. I even made that rug sale, and was back the next day for second helpings.

In the evenings, we'd hit the pubs in those towns for a sing-song 'round the old joanna and hope we didn't run into any husbands pissed that their wives were buying stuff on tick. Then back to King's Cross, load up and off again. Yep, we had a lot of laughs for three years.

There were bad payers. There always is. As I said, there was always more than one way to pay off a debt, but some women wouldn't go for it, or maybe the collector wouldn't. Most couldn't afford to pay off every week, but they'd keep things sweet – pay one week, miss the next. Hiding upstairs, behind the sofa. If a house or flat got into the red big-time, the collector would carve the letters RDS on a window-sill or door and you'd avoid it. I never did find out what those initials stood for.

Terry Underwood (left) and Alf (second left) at the Seafarers Club, Camden

Alf (far left) with his mates in the 1950s

On the road and on the knocker. (Alf far right)

A little later, I got a job up in Glasgow. Some job! Snatch-back. Repossession. The collectors for the credit companies were having a hard time. They weren't getting their money. Any money. I caught the overnight train up to Scotland. I slept in boarding houses during the night and repossessed gear during the day. I did this for about six months in the rough old tenements around the Mary Hill area. Dangerous but exciting. It was pretty much a fight every day. *Tap tap tap.* I never knew who was going to be on the other side of a door, a woman or a big fella. I always hoped it would be a little blonde with a warm bed looking for some company. But no matter how big the fella was, hit him on the side of the chin and he'll go. Hit with the knuckle.

Tap tap tap. I was out in a block of flats, near the top. The door opened, and – Jesus, that guy was *big*. Sweat-stained vest, probably once white. Fags and last night's whisky on his breath. "All right, Jock? You owe us a bit of money. Five pounds, this week." I knew nothing would work with this guy, but I went through the motions.

"Get ye the fuck outta my face."

This was going to end badly. I could see past the geezer into the flat. No furniture, a mattress on the floor, unwashed plates stacked on a broken sink. There was nothing in the place worth taking. Hang on. There, in the corner. Looked like a brand-new TV. Probably nicked, but I'll have it.

Then he started in, giving it some lip. "Who do ye think y'are, sonny? Come 'round here with ye fookin' book?"

I hit him. No one talks to me like that. I hit him again. He was one of those blokes who are all talk and no fight. He didn't even try to whack me, but somehow he got my thumb in his mouth and started chewing on it. That hurt. Now he was biting hard. I kept hitting him, and I'd peppered his face pretty good but I thought he was going to bite my thumb clean off. In the end, I grabbed him in a neck lock and squeezed. He let go, but my thumb looked like shit. I got that TV. He stood and watched, muttering, when I walked out with it, my thumb throbbing.

I met my wife on the knocker. We were knocking up Camberwell, in south London. I called on a house and Margaret answered. She was pumping gas at a local petrol station, but I thought she looked like Kim Novak. She wanted to get married. That was it, then – you meet, you get married. It was 1959. I was 24. I didn't want to get married, but it was

Alf in 1958 boarding a coach to Holland

about time I moved out of Ferdinand Road. Too many memories, not all good. I said, "Find us a place to live in and I'll marry you." Within a week, Margaret's sisters had found us a little rented flat. A sock of our own. Only trouble was, it was in south London. It was seen as traitorous for a north Londoner to move south of the Thames. It just didn't happen. South Londoners stayed in south London all their lives and us north Londoners never strayed below the river. Not permanently, anyway. Fuck it. This was my first house. OK, it was rented, but I kept my promise. We got married in the Sacred Heart Catholic Church in Camberwell and I moved into Hackford Road, off the Brixton Road. Angell Town, they call it. There was no money for a honeymoon.

There were plenty of gangs – teams, mobs, firms – operating in London then. Billy Hill and Jack Spot, two old-school gangsters who ran West End spielers and a web of protection rackets, had been the undisputed underworld kings. Spot was an extortionist and no slouch with a chiv – a razor taped so the blade didn't cut too deep, just enough for stitches. Down the cheek or striping down the leg and across the buttocks. Slash.

Terry Underwood and Alf (right) in Regent's Park in the 1950s

Alf and Margaret's wedding at the Sacred Heart Of Jesus Church, Camberwell, London, 31 October 1959

The Weavers' wedding day

Spot and Hill had run a war against each other, but their time was up. They were on the slide. Hill and his wife, Aggie – Ugly Aggie, we called her – had still got one or two clubs around town. But new men were on the up. In the East End, the Krays. The emerging team in south London was the Richardson gang, Charlie and Eddie. Eddie was a tough nut, and the brothers were also backed by hard men, all from around the Elephant and Castle. George Cornell – later shot dead by Ronnie Kray in the Blind Beggar pub – and Jimmy Moody.

Charlie and Eddie had been to school with Margaret's family and had their base, Peckford Scrap Metals, in New Church Road, near her house and just around the corner from our new gaff. Margaret knew Charlie well enough to invite him to our wedding. There wasn't any trouble at the wedding. No one would have dared.

The Richardsons had fearsome reputations. They were into one-armed bandits and fruit machines, protection and "the long game" – setting up a run of good credit with soap, rag, paper and other companies only to make one last big order on tick and disappear. The goods are then flogged on through pubs or street markets.

They were also into violence. Ultraviolence. The scrap yard became a venue for torture. Small-time cons and crooks who got on the wrong side of the Richardsons were given savage beatings at the Peckford yard. And not run-of-the mill beatings. Charlie and Eddie went in for an alternative dentistry service. No appointment necessary. They also had their own particular line in crucifixion. Victims were nailed to the floor. Hammer, hammer, hammer. There was also talk of an electric dynamo, which could send a nasty shock through some poor sod's balls. Twenty-four volts AC/DC. Not pleasant. Eventually, Charlie collected 25 years and Eddie drew a ten-stretch at their trial.

One of their top men was Frankie Fraser. Fraser had already earned himself a fierce rep as right hand to Hill. He was smaller than me, but was fearless. He'd weigh in with whatever was to hand – hammer, razor and, if there was tooth-pulling to be done at the Peckford yard, pliers. Fraser was also behind a particularly brutal slashing of Jack Spot. After that, the old villain got himself sewn up (it took over a hundred stitches) and went into retirement.

I saw quite a bit of Frankie. I'd see him around when we went drinking. Always had a word. Best to keep on his good side, just in case something went off. And it usually did, come the weekend. Some young thugs from Deptford or a new team around Borough would try and make a name for themselves.

I'd swerve it, if I could. On a night out with the wife and a couple of mates, there's better places to end up than the gutter in a fist-fight. There were pubs and clubs all around our manor and, if we felt like a big night, up west. Everything led up to Friday and Saturday nights. The George, Temple Bar, the Mason's Arms. Then down the Reform Club at the Elephant and Castle, or the Regency off the Walworth Road. Draughts, drinks, dancing, drunk – not always in that order. Sometimes the 51 Club on Charing Cross Road. The 49, on Brewer Street. And the Florida, off Leicester Square. Some great nights out, there.

I was still on the knocker, living day by day, week to week. I didn't tell Margaret too much about what I was doing. As long as there was money on the table come Friday. A few beers, a pack of fags – those were our luxuries.

I'd given up the boxing, but I used to go to Haringey Arena to watch fights. I'd go with Dennis. We used to buy the cheapest seats – at the back, a nicker a pop – but we'd always sit ringside. No one asked questions. Freddie Mills, Bruce Woodcock, I saw them all up at Haringey. Sometimes we'd go to Mile End Arena – I remember Mickey Duff boxing there – or to Hoxton Baths in Old Street or the Prince of Wales Baths in Kentish Town.

I was still playing football, in the Wood Green and District League. I didn't give it up until I was nearly 40. But I remember I did my cartilage. I'd torn it and carried on playing. University College Hospital did the operation. I was in for a month. Not just the hospital, but kept in bed so I didn't move. For a month. I'd get my friends to come 'round with weights so I could exercise my leg when the doctors weren't looking. There were some other distractions, too. A nurse took a bit of a shine to me and would get under the covers to give me head. You don't get that on the NHS.

Before betting went legit, in 1960, I also worked for street bookies up at the Angel, Islington. Bill McGuinness, Harry Bold, Mickey Flynn, they'd slip the local old bill half a note to keep them sweet. But some bobbies weren't on the take, or some bookies were just too mean to pay them off. Some of those guys got nicked time and again. I'd make a few shillings taking betting slips for them. I'd place the bets with bookies so I never had a wad on me if I got my collar felt. I must have been fined a dozen times, but I never got a record and could always go back if I wanted to earn a little extra.

I also worked with my brother's father-in-law, Tommy Tarr. He was a pitch bookie. We'd do Epsom, Ascot, Brighton, Sandown, all the big races. My job was to keep the books straight, to make sure Tommy wasn't giving more generous odds than the other bookies. I think he also had me around in case there was any strongarm work. The race gang wars were at their height and bookies were always getting carved up or sorted out if they didn't pay protection.

We used to drink in an Angel boozer called Spanish Pat's, a nice, old-style pub on Chapel Street market, off the Liverpool Road. Long gone, now. I got to know Robert Welch, Bobby, in Pat's. A big bastard. Hard, but clever with it. Always first with a round. Bobby was part of a firm of robbers. They'd been quite active, and he was always planning something, but you didn't ask. Bad form. Then one night I spotted Bobby in the Regency on the Walworth Road. I thought, That's odd. As I said, you rarely went off the manor to socialise, and certainly not south of the river. He was in thick with a crew from around the Elephant and gave me the brush off. I didn't recognise any of them, but I remember Bobby said he was there on some business, and I knew what that meant. The next I heard about Bobby, it was in *The Evening News*. Front page. The Great Train Robbery, the crime of the century. The names are now national folk heroes. Wisbey, Tommy Wisbey. Charlie Wilson, gunned down in Spain. Ronnie Biggs, still sunning himself in Rio. James, Roy James, was the driver. A great racing driver. Also dead. Goody, Hussey, White. Buster Edwards, the flower-seller. Killed himself. And Bruce Reynolds, the brains. They'd got away with over a million pounds from a mail train. Word had it there were a couple of other blokes on the job, but they were never caught. Bobby Welch had been in on it and he'd been arrested. Bobby didn't buy me another drink in Spanish Pat's. He got sent down for 30 years. Thirty years. Jesus. I wasn't even 30 myself. That was rough on Bobby.

I wasn't at the hospital when Margaret had our sons. Laurence came in 1963, Martin in 1966. Probably on the knocker or selling space. I suppose I wasn't a great father – particularly later, when I was on tour a lot – but we had a few holidays. Not in Spain, like everyone does nowadays; we were working class, and that meant England or Wales. Scotland at a push. I didn't know anyone who'd been abroad at that time, not even to Ireland. I'd passed my driving test in 1957 and had got a little A40. We'd drive down to Cornwall or the Isle of Wight, sometimes Tenby, in Wales. Anywhere that had a good little B&B. Full cooked breakfast – sausages, bacon (crispy bacon), eggs (two), beans, tomatoes and a couple of rounds of fried bread. A couple of mugs of coffee, piping hot. Toast and marmalade, thick-cut. Margaret had strawberry jam. Lovely.

I was married with kids. I didn't want to get mixed up with gangs, but I didn't mind having a word with anyone into the old lemon lime. As I said, I liked Fraser, and sometimes I'd run into Hill, the self-styled boss of the London underworld. He sat in the background and let all his goons do the heavy work. He was always dropping hints about jobs he was involved in – crimes committed, that sort of thing. Bit of a bighead, Billy.

But the thing about Billy was, he liked his music, so he wasn't all bad. We used to chat about the latest tunes whenever we caught up. He liked Sinatra – 'Fly Me To The Moon' – a bit of Dean Martin. I did, too: "Fly me to the moon, fly me to the moon." One night, I was down at a club in Brixton, the Beehive. Quite classy for the neighbourhood. A spieler. I was with Charlie, one of Margaret's brothers. Charlie was getting himself a reputation as a bit of a tough and had been in on a fight at some other club around the Elephant a few nights before. Someone had got hurt. His mates wanted to settle the score.

The Weaver family in the 1960s

The Beehive wasn't busy that night. Charlie was drinking at a table with a group of friends. There was a couple smooching and I was at the bar, passing the time with Billy Hill. We were talking Frankieverymuch. "I'm telling you, Billy, the Capitol years were Sinatra's landmark. That was a bloody landmark." In comes this team of heavy bastards looking for Charlie. What did they use for ambushes in those days? Knives and chivs, of course, but also truncheons, lead pipe, spanners, starting handles. Sometimes wrapped in shirts, sometimes not. I didn't see what they hit me with. I didn't even see them walk in, but I'm certain Hill did. Did he know what was going to happen? Maybe. We just kept talking. "You're wrong, Alf. Sinatra was at his best with 'New York, New York'." And then, *crunch* – I got a whack in the jaw. They broke it. They wanted me out of the way and they managed that. I don't remember much else about it, but I ended up unconscious outside on the pavement. They beat the shit out of Margaret's brother. He was in hospital for weeks. That battering gave me something else to live with: sugar diabetes. "Thanks, Charlie," I said. "Thanks a lot."

I didn't find out about the diabetes for some time. I was selling local directories at the time for a firm called Kemp's in King's Cross. The game was to get people to sign up. We'd say, "Do you want to be in the directory again next year?" They'd always say no. These were useless things. We'd say, "OK, can you sign here, where it says 'I don't want to be in it'?" Then Kemp's would sell those names on to some other firm. It was a hot summer and I was losing weight. I was eating but not gaining anything. I'd be on the scales every day. Eleven and a half stone. I'd eat more. Eleven. I drank more. More Guinness. Ten and a half stone. I still went down, right down to nine stone nine. I was smoking, had been since I was 15. Forty-a-day habit. Senior Service, untipped, then Kent, now B&H. I thought, Jesus, I've got cancer! The doctors did some tests and put me on insulin and I've been on it every day since, one shot in the morning, one shot before my evening meal, either in my legs or in my stomach, if I'm in a restaurant. That was nearly 40 years ago. Thanks, Charlie. Thanks a lot.

4 An Old Beatles Car

We were getting by but going nowhere fast. It was 1965. I was 30, for Christ's sake, and The Beatles had already released eleven singles and nine EPs. They were working on *Rubber Soul*, out later that year. The birth of pop music hadn't had that much impact on me. Maybe I was too old. John Lennon and Ringo were five years younger than me. George Harrison was eight years younger. They were a different generation.

I don't remember buying any of those early Beatles singles. Not 'Love Me Do', not 'She Loves You', not 'I Want To Hold Your Hand'. They'd played Walthamstow's Granada and the London Palladium in 1963, Finsbury Park's Astoria in 1964 and Hammersmith Odeon in 1965. I missed them all, but I knew who The Beatles were. Who didn't? They were the biggest group in the world. I heard the songs 'Please Please Me' and 'From Me To You' on the radio. They also played those 45s down the Regency.

Then my sister Ann starting going steady with a guy called Ronnie. He was a market man with a fruit-and-veg stall up Camden way. Snowy-white mush. Nanas, bananas. He also had a sister, June. She was going out with this bloke, Don Murfet. Murfet had once worked for NEMS, North End Music Stores, the Liverpool record chain run by The Beatles' manager, Brian Epstein. Now he was out on his own, running a firm near my old stomping ground on Inverness Street. Artist Car Services. Cars for celebs. Chauffeurs to the stars. No one was doing anything like this then.

Ann told me that Murfet was looking to hire. I hadn't nailed a steady job and was tiring of life on the knocker. What could I lose? Murfet had somehow got hold of the huge old Austin Princess that The Beatles had used on their tours. A big car. He was trying to drum up work with American singers and groups over to play a few dates around England.

Don Murfet (right)

That seemed like a good idea. Cushy, too. How hard could it be to swan around in a car? I was also a little bit impressed that Murfet had managed to buy himself a car from the *A Hard Day's Night* group. I caught the Northern Line north. Back in Camden, I joined up. Then I got myself kitted out for the job.

The tailors in those days were John Stephen on Carnaby Street and The Beatles' favourite, Dougie Millings, on Great Pulteney Street, who kitted out everyone from Cliff Richard to Warren Beatty. Bespoke suits. Better than Savile Row, but a heavy wedge and out of my league. I used to go to Toby Norman. He did a nice line in £30 whistles and had a shop up in Wood Green. I was always a suit man. People looked up to you if you turned up suited and booted. People would take notice of you. Single-breasted, narrow lapel. A little later, double-breasted, cut high, and always fitted. Very fitted. I always liked looking smart. I'd look at Sinatra and Martin, the whole Rat Pack look, and copy their style. We were all very well dressed. Not flash but smart. I always hung my suits up when I came in, no matter how boozed I was. I also wore Italian-style shoes, hand-made from a shop off the Tottenham Court Road and highly polished. Spit and rub, spit and rub – a shiny pair of one and twos. That was a hangover from my army days. They also did a two-inch Cuban heel, which just gave me that little bit extra.

The stars – and work – were thin on the ground to start with. Maybe once or twice in a week we'd drive the Princess to Heathrow Airport and pick up whoever was coming into town. We'd drive back to London, check them into a hotel, onto a restaurant or a club in the evening. Maybe we'd spin them around for a week and then check them out and back to the airport. It all worked well, unless two acts were in town, like Bobby Darin and The Four Tops.

This is how it went. I'd drive the Princess. Don would follow in his battered little Triumph. I'd swing the limo into the West End and pick Bobby up from Claridges. Then into Soho to drop him off for dinner at Bianchi's, on Frith Street. While Bobby gets his chops around a three-courser, I'd swap cars with Don. He'd steam down to the Dorchester to collect The Four Tops with me behind, this time in the Triumph. Drop The Four Tops off at the Scotch of St James. Swap cars. I'm back to Bobby, who's just finished off the profiteroles and is tucking into the brandy. With one decent car between us, we kept this up for the best part of a year and never got caught.

Artist Car Services started to get a name for itself. We were good drivers. Safe. We knew the streets, and we knew the clubs. The 51 Club, 'round the corner of Coventry Street, then up Greek Street to the Establishment Club. That was run by Peter Cook. The $7^1/_2$ Club in the West End. The Flamingo. The Blarney. The Ad Lib, a little club on Leicester Place, just by the old Empire cinema. It was run by Brian Morris, who went out with Alma Cogan. In the lift and *boom!* The music hit you. James Brown – 'Out Of Sight', 'Papa's Got A Brand New Bag'. Otis Redding – 'Mr Pitiful', 'I've Been Loving You Too Long'. Aretha Franklin – 'Respect', "Give it to me."

Swinging London started here. The Beatles were always there, and The Rolling Stones. Then there were the beautiful people – models, designers, Mary Quant, shopgirls from Granny Takes A Trip, Ossie Clark, hairdressers, Vidal Sassoon. Some of the young managers, Andrew Loog Oldham, and The Faces – John Dunbar, Marianne Faithfull, Anita Pallenberg. It was a great buzz. There was a bird down there, a transsexual, one of the first. I always found out the best places and clubs through asking around. You had to have somewhere. Then, when someone hit town, it'd be, "Right, where's hot, Alf? Where can I pull a bird?" And I'd say, "We're going down the Ad Lib." You could always pick up a bird at the Ad Lib. They loved it.

Bodyguards, heavies, minders and security didn't really exist at this time for pop and rock stars. They took their chances and the police took most of the stick. Fans always wanted a piece, and they were wanting bigger and bigger pieces. They'd go mad, absolutely crazy with The Beatles. They'd bang the car or throw themselves on the bonnet. Someone was always making a grab, so pushing through a crowd with a singer on your arm just became another part of the job of driving them around. We'd open the car door, take them from the car to the club or restaurant. I'd keep my eye open for nutters. It became instinctive, even at clubs. I'd go inside, if we were at a club or another place the public had access to. I began to notice some of the other drivers would have a few drinks, ease off and joke around a bit – remember, no one had told us to get heavy – but I'd stay alert if I was with someone. I didn't want them getting mobbed all day and then all night as well, and I'm damn sure they didn't. Just one whisky, straight up. Keep alert. Anyone came over looked like they were going to be trouble, *whack*. Nothing too hard. A slap, really, just so they'd notice and not get too familiar. Not everyone was going to get this. Blondes with all the right parts and who knew what to do with them were never going to be a problem. A little bit of boxing, common sense and one drink. Two, tops. It got me a long way, and I was getting good at it, sorting out trouble, smoothing the way. People were beginning to ask for me.

I'd met a guy, Frank Fenter. He worked at Atlantic Records and was bringing the Stax tour over to London. Eddie Floyd, Carla Thomas, Otis Redding, Booker T And The MG's.

Monday 13 March	Meet Stax tour at airport
Wednesday 15 March	Stax press reception, Speakeasy Club
Saturday 18 March	Stax tour at Upper Cut Club

We picked them up from the airport and they were straight down the clubs. They loved the clubs. There was always the Scotch – the Scotch of St

James, in Mason's Yard, 'round the corner from Jermyn Street. You were vetted through a sliding window. Quick peep. "Otis. Hey, Otis is here." We're in. There was tartan all over the place and the music was loud. Very loud. The record company took all the records down there and the DJ would spin them. All the Stax acts loved that, and so did every other rock star in London. They all inhabited the Scotch. If you weren't at the Scotch, you weren't part of the scene. I saw Tom Jones down there, Eric Burdon from The Animals, Rod Stewart, The Moody Blues and the Stones. And The Beatles, of course.

Then we'd take them down the Bag O'Nails – up Duke Street, right on Piccadilly, left on Sackville Street, right at Vigo, cross Regent Street, into Beak and left onto Kingly Street. Number eight. Down into the basement. Down at the Bag. Drinking and dancing. Down at the Bag. Sometimes steak and chips. Down at the Bag. I'd phone up in advance and tell them we were coming. "Alf Weaver here," I'd say.

"Alf, my man. What can we do for you?" I was getting known as the man who looked after these stars.

"I've got Sam And Dave. We're coming down, all right?"

Knock, knock. "Yuh?"

"It's Alf."

Bolts off, door opens. Down at the Bag. "OK, man. Come on through. Hey, Sam, my man. Yeah, Dave. How's it going? Drink?" I liked that. Sam And Dave were incredible dancers. I tried to copy a few moves, but it was impossible. I'd left it too late to learn some of those steps. Those guys had stuff going on that we'd never dreamt of, down the Regency. Down at the Bag, they also had a tiny stage and live music. Some of the new bands – Jimi Hendrix – played there. I got Margaret and my friends into the clubs, too, and because they were with me they'd be looked after. I never paid for a meal all those years. "On the house, Alf. Your money's no good here. My treat, fella." They knew that I'd bring in any new group that came to town, so it was good for business.

I remember I took Otis Redding down to Brixton during the Stax tour. a little drinking club, where he performed. The Ram Jam Club, SW9. He was never going to be in trouble, but I could have been. I remember the night well. I was the outsider, the only white face in that joint. But Otis stuck with it, didn't let me out of his sight. And while I with Otis, I was down with "the man". I was suddenly the coolest white man in Brixton. Made a change from my last big showing down there, getting a beating at the Beehive.

I liked Otis a lot. He was quiet. Real quiet. Maybe shy, and nothing like his stage show, which was 100 per cent full-on, rocket-fuel stuff. I remember standing at the back of that club. The songs were blasting out, coming at us fast and loose – 'Satisfaction', 'These Arms Of Mine', 'I've Been Loving You Too Long'. I hadn't moved but my shirt was covered in sweat. It was *hot* in there. Redding looked like he could party all night. And we did. The last time I saw him, we were weaving down Electric Avenue with dawn just coming up. Just two soul brothers. He was dead within two years. What a tragedy.

Artist Cars were getting more work. Johnny Mathis was another one of the early names we did. Always smart, Johnny. He had some lovely shirts – dinner shirts, frills in pink, purple, plum. He always wore them with black trousers, wool but lightweight, very tapered. He was playing the Prince of Wales in Coventry Street one week. But Mathis was a strange one. He hated the fans. Couldn't bear them near him. When the curtain came down, that was it, he was off. Almost sprinted off the stage. I'd be ready in the wings. All his gear was already stashed in the limo and we'd sprint out the back door of the theatre and away. "Come on, Alf. Foot down. Step on it. Let's get out of here." We'd be on Piccadilly before the audience stopped applauding and nearly at Hyde Park Corner by the time they were out of the stalls and hunting for a G&T and Johnny's autograph. He'd sit in the back of the Princess tearing at his tie.

During the run, Johnny was renting a house just off Park Lane. Nice place, very swank. The first night I worked for him, we got back to his place. John ducks inside and I start humping his bags up the stairs to his bedroom. In I go. Fuckin' hell! Mathis is standing there stark bollock naked. Just standing there. Probably thought I was a nice bit of rough. A bit old, maybe, but I was still in shape. OK, here we go, I thought. I knew he was a bit King Lear. An iron. A back-door merchant. It was no big secret. But it's a funny old thing when Johnny Mathis – singing star, idol to thousands of blue rinses – puts the moves on you, so I said, "John, forget it." He was still standing there without his strides. "Look, I'm straight. I ain't no fairy, and I don't care if I lose my job or not, because I'm fucking straight, all right?" Christ, I was married. Two kids. Now I'm shouting. "Right, I'm off. See you." I'd like to say I walked out of there cool and calm, but I was down those stairs like a shot, two or three at a time, and out the door. Had a couple of smokes in the car. First bloke makes a pass at me and it's Johnny fucking Mathis giving me the eye. But to be fair, John had just said, "OK. Sorry, Alf. It was worth a go, though, wasn't it?" Fair play to the fella. Most try it on with the female help. There was no follow-up. In fact, I must have worked with John for years, on and off, and we were fine after that. Actually, we laughed about it every time we met. The poofter and the boxer. A pretty unlikely match.

Who else did we do in those days? Matt Monro. I used to drop in on Matt. Matt was a great guy. Lovely fella. He had a house up in Hampstead, and he'd invite us all up there for a cup of tea and a packet of Digestives. "Hello, son. How you doing?" Matt was a bus driver before he got into the singing game with the lyricist Don Black, the guy who wrote 'Born Free'. Matt drove the old Routemasters through the East End. Number 27. *Ding, ding.* Tickets please. Yeah, Matt was very down to earth. He was a sort of British Frank Sinatra, but success never changed him. It was always tea and cake with Matt, never diamonds, fur coats and champagne. People would take notice of you.

We also worked with Donovan. I loved him. A nice guy. Gypsy Dave was always with him, a friend. He bought a house in Wentworth, Surrey, near the golf course down there. He was always real close to his old man, as I remember. He was a terrific Scottish guy. Donovan had a swimming pool, and we all lazed in the sun while he played the guitar. Five or six of us would be hanging around. Donovan would try out a few chords. *Dee dah dah dee.* Nice little tune. We'd shout out if he'd got something – "Yeah, like that. I like that." Us in the pool and Donovan on the strings. Those were fun afternoons.

Monday 2 January	Went to Matt Monro's house
Tuesday 3 January	Took Matt's wife, Mickey, shopping
Wednesday 4 January	Dropped Mickey Monro at station – to Manchester to see Matt
Monday 9 January	Don Black home, Matt Monro to South Africa, Mickey Monro to New York

Sunday 15 January	Donovan concert, Royal Albert Hall
Thursday 19 January	Matt's house with Donovan

That old Beatles car was beginning to see a lot of action and a lot of stars. We had some nobodies in the back seat, too, but who can remember them?

One time, I went down to Epsom to pick up a guitarist and give him a bit of boost at a gig. It turned out to be Jeff Beck. Eric Clapton, old slow hand, had just quit The Yardbirds and Beck had taken over the guitar-hero spot. But he wasn't famous yet. No one had heard of him. Just another hot-shot guitarist. 'Hi-Ho Silver Lining' was still a tune in his head, and Jeff was staying over at his old ma and pa's place, in a block of flats. Up I come in the Princess limo. Jeff sticks his head out of a window and shouts, "Here, Mum, they've sent a bleedin' limo!" He couldn't believe it. "A great big fucking limousine! And it's mine!" Steady, Jeff. It was only the Princess.

I drove him down to Kingston, and he wouldn't shut up about the car. Kept going on about it. "Look at the leather trim, man. Blimey! Rosewood dash!" I don't think Becky had been in too many cars.

A year later, he was out of The Yardbirds. That was the next time I caught up with them. Beck was out and Page was in – Jimmy Page, another guitar hero. Beck had been kicked out by the rest of the band, Chris Dreja, Keith Relf – he was a great singer, fantastic on the old harp – and Jim McCarty on the skins. They'd all had it with Beck. Jimmy, too. This was early 1967 and the word was that Beck was putting another little group together. I got a call.

Saturday 13 May	Jeff Beck to Drill Hall, Kingston
Tuesday 30 May	Pick up Jeff Beck from Sutton

Some shack Beck was playing at. A scrubby little drill hall where the army boys did their stuff, a long way from the big theatres Beck had been playing with The Yardbirds. Maybe they thought it was going to cut up a bit rough with a bunch of squaddies in the room. That's what I was there for. Here we go, I thought. Some other group Beck was playing in. Few get more than two bites at the business. One-hit wonder or two-time loser? And can I keep him out of trouble?

It was sweaty and loose in there. I remember standing at a makeshift bar, a few cans of beer on a decorator's table. One kid had had more than enough of the barley wine by the time we pitched up and started giving me some mouth, probably because I was wearing a whistle. I gave him a slapping. There was always some fucking about at gigs like this. Then the group's out. Jeff, Ron Wood on bass (saw him again with the Stones), Dunbar on drums. And Jeff's doing the business – 'You Shook Me', 'I Ain't Superstitious'. And then I notice the singer. Little guy, swinging his mike all over the fucking place. Rod Stewart. Little Rodney. But he had a great voice, really strong, and the place just stopped, listening. This was how The Jeff Beck Group got its first break, in a sweaty little drill hall down Kingston way. I bumped into Eric Clapton and the rest of Cream a few days later and told them Beck was back in business.

I also got friendly with Bobby Darin. Robert Cassotto, that was his real name. From the Bronx, but a great fella and a hit with the bubblegum brigade. Remember 'Splish Splash'? Bobby was over in England making a film. I'm giving him the tour, keeping the ladies out of his face. So here we go. We're spinning around Berkeley Square. Bobby loved his posh, all the Mayfair noshers, the Park Lane casinos.

Bob sees a Roller dealer. "Here, Alf. Let's take ourselves in there for a peep." We ball in and Bobby clocks one of the motors, the biggest bleedin' car in there. Coffee-coloured, all the trimmings. One of the salesmen comes over and Bob goes, "I like that Silver Cloud. How much is that?" Now, Bobby has been the biggest-earning pop star in the world, by this time. He'd done 'Mack The Knife', for Christ's sake, his signature tune. 'Dream Lover'. Was married to Sandra Dee. But this lemon in the showroom doesn't know that. Thinks we're a pair of wides trying it on. Gives us the look, down his nose. "I'm sorry, sir," he snots. "You simply won't be able to afford that." Bob looks the guy over but didn't say a dicky, just walked out. Turned and went. I looked the dumb prick over. "Yes, sir? Can I help you?" He's giving me the full look now. Thinks I'm something he's trodden on.

"Do you know who that was?" I asked. The chinless one blanks. "That was Bobby Darin. And you just said goodbye to him. He could buy this motor, that motor" – I'm pointing now – "that motor, that one. In fact, he could buy the whole goddamn place and you besides." The bloke's face dropped big-time. He'd just lost the easiest sale he was ever going to make and he knew it.

A few years later, Bobby started calling himself Bob, Bob Darin, and swapped his sharp duds for a pair of Levis and love beads. Dylan was going electric, Darin was going acoustic. This was his folk song, his "give the kids a message" bit. I didn't think it suited him and nor did the fans, but we still kept in touch. We were a right pair of letter writers: "Dear Bobby, I've just been listening to *Their Satanic Majesties Request* by The Rolling Stones. '2,000 Light Years From Home' reminded me of you..." A week or so later and a Yank-stamped airmailer would drop onto my south London mat. "Dear Alf. Why don't you drive by that Rolls Royce dealer and tell him to kiss my ass? Kiss my big fat American-pie ass..." Sense of humour, our Bob.

He had a couple of real blows. One, he found out his sister was really his mom. Wow! That would tear anyone in half. Two, Robert Kennedy was shot. *Pow*. That really busted him apart. He wrote he'd gotten into politics big-time in the late '60s – Vietnam and all that – but Bobby knew the score. He'd come up from nothing, like me. He told me all about Robert Kennedy. The two Bobbys were going to put America right again. Then Kennedy was shot and Bobby jacked it all in and moved to California, Big Sur.

One day, in the early '70s, I got a call from Bobby from the States: "Alf, Bobby Darin." By this time he'd dropped the Bob stuff. "I'm going back to the old ways, get the cabaret threads out of storage. I need someone I can trust. Are you in?" I had to tell him no. I'd just got back from a long stay in the States myself and Margaret wouldn't go for it. The way I heard it, he did get back to something like his old self, playing Vegas and places. Then the next I heard, he was dead, in '73. He'd been really affected by Kennedy's death. I think that took his future away and shook him up. It also took his heart away. He was 37. No age. That was a shame.

One thing I'll never forget about Bobby was how generous he was. When he was leaving to go back to the US the first time I worked with him, he wrote out a cheque and pressed it into my hand when we shook goodbye. I might get thrown a few quid cash or a bottle of Jameson's if I'd done all right. A good job meant no hassle, no fights, no nothing. Bobby had no complaints. Smooth as silk, working for him. So I glanced down at this Bank of America cheque. Looked like 50 nicker. Christmas was coming and Alf could put a good-sized bird on the table and sort out presents with that. Hey, thanks, Bobby. But when I got home, I unfolded the cheque and could see there were two noughts after the five, not one. He'd made it out for a monkey, half what I was then earning in a year. Christmas was going to be the best. Thanks, Bobby! Thank you very much, Mr Darin. I knew I was never going to get any money out of Sonny And Cher.

That diary again:

Friday 20 January 1967   Sonny and Cher arrive from USA

Sonny was a fucking weirdo. Tight-fisted, too. A real mean bastard. I didn't like him one bit. I thought Cher could probably do better on her own. Seemed like a nice girl, but that was their thing. He was really into himself. Never said two words to anyone, certainly not please and thank you. Little runt with a monk hairdo. He thought he was too cool, a cut above the rest. And they were always having rows in the back of the car. They'd have a right old bull, always shouting and screaming at each other.

Sometimes Sonny would put the divide up between the front and back seats, but I could still hear them at it, screaming and shouting. We'd get to the show and suddenly it would go all quiet. Not a squeak. Eammon Andrews or some other show host would bowl over and they'd be all smiles and kisses. "Hello. Oh, lovely. How are you?" They'd do the interview. "Oh, we love each other." Then back in the car and *bang*, the arguments would start over again. But that's showbiz.

One day I get a job down at Tilbury Docks, down by the river. A bunch of guys and their families were coming in from Australia. The whole family, on a boat. Must have taken weeks. I was waiting by the car and these teeth are coming down the gangplank under a pile of suitcases. It was The Bee Gees, looking green – except for those teeth, of course – and totally unknown, carrying all this luggage and a whole load of furniture – sideboards, wardrobes, lamps. Everything but the kitchen sink, but maybe that too. I took them up to some house in Hendon, nothing special. A bit of a dump, to tell the truth. "See you.

And good luck." They'd need it, I thought. Be back in Oz before the end of the week. I wasn't right about everything. But it was all down to an old Beatles car.

5 Monkeemania

On 11 September 1966, something happened in America: the first public performance by The Monkees aired. A day later, the group's TV series premièred on NBC. The similarities with *A Hard Day's Night* were not accidental; it was a direct rip-off. Hollywood director Bob Rafelson and producer Bert Schneider had run an ad in *The Hollywood Reporter* looking for four kids under 21: "Wanted: Ben Franks types." What they really wanted was another John, Paul, George and Ringo. What they got was the fab four of George Michael Dolenz, Robert Michael Nesmith, Peter Thorkelson and Davy Jones, The Monkees. I heard they turned down another young hopeful. Charles Manson wouldn't forget the snub.

England had had The Beatles, and now America had their own group. A bit of a result. Within months, they were a success. 'Last Train To Clarksville' in October 1966. 'I'm A Believer', their only UK Number One single, at the end of the same year. And then they were in England, and I was going to look after them. They were booked into the Royal Garden Hotel, overlooking Hyde Park. I picked up Mike and Davy from the airport, rushed them through and back to the hotel. Their rooms overlooked the park, and fans were already out there. They would be out waiting at six in the morning. They'd wait all day. If they felt like it, The Monkees would wave to them. Sometimes they didn't bother. The kids would still wait. This was my first taste of Monkeemania. I couldn't understand it. I'd seen Beatlemania, although not up close like this, but I was getting the hang of it. People would just go nuts. Not excitable. Not ecstatic. Not exuberant. Nuts. We got a couple of bruisers to help out, keep the kids from coming into the hotel. There was a few pints in it for them.

It felt like something was happening, and for the first time I felt part of it. I was right at the centre. I liked Mike straight off. He was a Texan. He was the oldest of the group and just seven years younger than me. I was like his older brother, and we got along just fine. It was also his first time in England. Davy was from Manchester. He was already a soap star, as Ena Sharples' grandson in *Coronation Street*, in *Z Cars* – remember the theme tune? *duh, der, der, duh, der, der, der, duh* – and later in the West End, as the Artful Dodger in *Oliver!*. But the rest of the band were hungry for the sights. Mike wanted to see all of London, and we'd sneak past the kids lounging in Hyde Park to take in Buck Palace, the Houses of Parliament, Big Ben, Westminster Abbey and Tower Bridge.

We had a couple of days of this and then they had to do what they had come over for: concerts. This was their first appearance in England, and they were nervous. "Hey, Alf, what are the fans like?" That was Mike. "Look out the window, mate." Davy next: "Do you think we're as good as The Beatles?" Jesus. "Yeah, easy." What was I going to say? I don't think they believed me.

The first gig was the Arena in Wembley, west London. A bit of a dump, in those days, but not a bad start. I was still technically hired as a driver or, as I liked to say, chauffeur. Nowadays there are drivers, who drive, and minders, who do the minding. It's separate. Two different jobs, professionally done. But in the old days, we did everything, driving and minding. I liked it. There were few rules, but what there were I was making up as we went along.

I took The Monkees up to the gig together. They were in the back, apprehensive but also putting on a front, clowning around. Mickey was the joker in the pack. Mad Mickey. Into their uniforms – another Beatles steal – and onto the stage. The whole place was screamed down. Sometimes a sort of chant went up: "Monkeeezz! Monkeeezz!" One or two girls – they were all girls, tiny teenage schoolkids – screamed out for their favourite. Mostly that meant Davy. He was the favourite. "Daveeeeeee!" Mickey hit the drums. The screaming just got louder. The first song The Monkees played on UK soil was 'Last Train To Clarksville'. I didn't hear it – I couldn't hear a thing over the screaming – but Mike told me after that they always hit off with that one. After that, it was more screaming and then it went something like 'She's So Far Out (She's In)', 'You Just May Be The One', 'I Wanna Be Free', 'Take A Giant Step', 'Sweet Young Thing', 'Papa Gene's Blues', 'Do Not Ask For Love', 'I Can't Get Her Off My Mind', 'Mary, Mary', 'Cripple Creek', 'You Can't Judge A Book By Looking At The Cover', 'Gonna Build A Mountain', 'IGA Woman', 'I'm A Believer' and '(I'm Not Your) Stepping Stone'. Then they were off. The screaming didn't give up. *Aaaaaaggggggghhhhh!* I hadn't expected this. Kids were fainting all over the place. They were dragged to the back, where they had all these camp-beds set up. They'd be up and back screaming within the minute. I was always on the side of the stage. Some girls were getting up there, running at Davy, sometimes Mickey. I'd run out and pull them off, drop them back into the audience. Then they'd be up again. If we saw a kid faint, we'd drag her out and put her backstage. Then we realised they were feigning the faint. As soon as they were on the camp-bed backstage, they'd jump up and rush the stage. Up. Down. Back in the crowd. Faint. Up. Down again. It was non-stop. All through this, the screaming never stopped. *Aaaaaaggggggghhhhh!* "I'm a believer." This was unbelievable.

That first night, we weren't prepared for the getaway. They couldn't go out the front. "Monkeeezz! Monkeeezz!" They'd be ripped to shreds. Leaving a gig nowadays is organised like a military operation – exits are checked, roads are scouted and a plan is formulated – but we were learning on the hoof at Wembley in 1966. "Monkeeezz! Monkeeezz!" The group were looking at me. They were used to fans but not fanatics. "Forget the limo, boys, and hop in the van." I was talking about a beaten-up old van we had used to bring some of the boys over. Mickey, Peter, Davy and Mike piled in without complaint. They weren't keen to go out front. "Monkeeezz! Monkeeezz!" We covered them with a couple of coats and some blankets, slammed the doors shut and out the side entrance. Jimmy Saville had compered the gig, and now I saw him outside, mopping up the atmosphere. "Here, Jim. Get over here." I got the disc jockey into the limo. He was the decoy. The limo had smoked glass, making it impossible to see in, and we inched out into the crowd of screaming kids.

Everyone was going mad. OK, nuts. They were hammering on the bonnet, on the doors, on the windows. *Bang, bang, bang.* It was scary. I didn't envy The Monkees this. I thought the windows were going to come in. We were making 1mph, maybe less, inching through this crowd, and every foot the car would be hammered with tiny fists. Inside, it sounded like thunder. Inside, we were panicking.

"Open the window, Jimmy," I shouted. I wanted Saville to show his mug, show the crowd that The Monkees weren't in the car. Maybe they'd leave us alone. But DJ Saville had his own ideas. Maybe he thought the kids were there for him. He wound the window down two inches and poked his fingers out. Now-then, now-then, why-do-you-want-me-to-open-this-here-window? It-is-cold-outside. How's-about-that, guys-and-gals? The kids went nuts squared. They thought those fingers were Davy's, or Mickey's. Mike's, even. "Open the fucking window, Jimmy. Let them see us." That was me again. Saville wound the window down and the kids fell back when they saw the white hair and cigar. They weren't interested in mobbing a disc spinner. Times change.

That was my first experience of Monkeemania or anything like it. Kids have shouted for other groups over the years, but it has never reached that fever pitch again. I've also not forgotten how frightening a 16-year-old kid with a big scream can be.

There were four more Monkee shows to do. We were back on the A40, following the boys back into London, and the cold air was blasting us through the open car window. "Shut that bloody window, will you, Jimmy?"

It's not like I had the rest of the evenings off. Most of them were spent with The Monkees down the Cromwellian, a dancing, drinking, eating, gambling, anything-goes sort of place opposite the Natural History Museum, in Kensington. A bit moody. I'd call up, give them some rabbit: "How would you like The Monkees at your establishment?" All the booze would be laid on. The birds, too.

It was always packed with the Chelsea mob – maybe McCartney, sometimes Lennon or another Beatle or two. This is where Davy came into his element. He fixed the social calendar. I guess it was his country. Davy could be irritating. That grin could sure get tiresome. But I liked him. He meant well, and it wasn't his fault he was only five-five. He and Mike, who was pushing a good foot taller than his bandmate, looked like the Odd Couple. Davy had been an apprentice jockey in his youth, and we used to talk racing during any downtime. He gave me a few good tips on the horses: "Morning Star, down from three to one to evens. Get in now or you'll be too late." Often as not, he'd be right. Should have got a job for *The Sporting Life*. As a favour, I'd bell some stables I knew up by Lancaster Gate and get Davy fixed up with a ride around Hyde Park.

Davy didn't need help fixing himself with a ride at the Cromwellian. He thought the light poured out of him. He was always on the pull, and rarely failed, despite his lack of inches. A real ladies' man. Cromwellian, champagne, cop. Every night. It was difficult not to score. Peter and Mickey were up for it, too, although Mike was married and didn't chase around.

Inevitably, sometimes there would be more skirt than could go around the four boys. That was a perk of the job, a kiss and a cuddle, but I had to be careful. I was doing a job. Even in a limp-wristed joint like the Cromwellian, there was always someone loaded on brandy and valium out to cause a scene. We had a couple of dicey moments. Girls would come over to chat to Mickey and Davy. Their boyfriends would follow and give it a bit of lip. Nothing I couldn't handle. Someone always needed a slapping. I used to say, "If you start anything, it'll be the last thing you do. Get rid of the girlfriend."

My diabetes meant I kept a check on my drinking. A glass of wine, make it last all night. In a ten-hour shift, nothing would happen, but I'd look away for a minute and there'd be a daisy in a pair of candy-coloured strides wanting to cause some trouble for Mickey.

Mad Mickey, he was always looning. The joker who was crap at drums. He hated playing them. He hooked up with the bird from *Jukebox Jury*, pretty early on, and I didn't see much of him from then. Peter was pretty square. He didn't seem to fit. A real miserable sod. I'm not sure the rest of the band had much time for him, either, and some nights I'm sure they'd make an effort to lose him or leave him behind at the hotel.

As I said, I got on best with Mike. A bit of a loner, behind all the Monkee bullshit that was going on. There was also more going on with Mike. He was the driving force of the band, the real muso, the lead guitarist with the tunes and the lyrics, and he was always up for meeting other musicians on the London scene, although he was always embarrassed that he was a Monkee, from a manufactured group who played bubblegum pop. And he was a country music fan, born and raised in the Big Country. He hated it, especially the hype. He'd have preferred to be a Beatle or a Stone or in any other band. I remember introducing him to the Stones. Bill Wyman was always in a dark club corner, probably on the prowl, looking for skirt. But at least he was a real bassist. Mike often complained that there weren't any musicians in The Monkees, just a bunch of puppets who got session men in to help them record. He'd get depressed and we'd hit the streets or go for a drive, do the London tour again – Big Ben, Tower Bridge – and Mike could pretend he wasn't a Monkee. I saw Mike again in 1967, when he and his wife, Phyllis, were in London on vacation.

Mike desperately wanted an in with the hip scene. I knew he was in awe of John Lennon. Thought he was a serious artist, not a puppet. Lennon got

Mike Nesmith and his wife, Phyllis

a haircut, Mike copied him. Lennon got a Mini Cooper, Mike got one. Lennon got a white Rolls Royce, Mike got a white…er…Cadillac. Nearly, Mike. Now he wanted an in with his hero. I'd done some work on and off with The Beatles in the last year or so and had got to know all the boys down at Apple, the three right-hand men of the fab four: Mal Evans, Pete Brown and Neil Aspinall. I could get Mike that in.

Just by luck, the BBC wanted The Beatles to feature in its live, global broadcast *Our World* on 25 June. "Here, Pete, listen. You know, Mike Nesmith is a huge Beatles fan. What about us coming down?" No problem. We were in. Mike was in. Come the day, I picked up Mike and Phyllis and we all packed into Studio One at Abbey Road. Mick Jagger, Keith Richards and Brian Jones were all there, the holy trinity of the Stones. So was Eric Clapton, The Who's loon Keith Moon and Jagger's bird, Marianne Faithfull. And Mike, of course. Everyone was sporting full flower-power – beads, paisley shirts, gypsy waistcoats, velvet pants, purple anything and everything. That's everyone apart from me and producer George Martin, the suit men, grey flannel with white shirts. The whole place was buzzing.

Suddenly Lennon in his full psychedelic trip was next to us. "Hey, John. This is Mike Nesmith. Mike, John Lennon." Lennon was pretty cool. "Oh, yeah. Mike. I love The Monkees." A fucking problem for Mike. He hated the group, but his hero loved them. Could he start to love his own group? No. But they got on well enough.

Then there was a big hush and we waited for the seconds to tick down before the show went live. Five, four, three, two, one. And then the band unveiled this fantastic new song, 'All You Need Is Love'. I'd never heard it before. Me and Mike were singing along, although I didn't know the words. Still don't. "All you need is love." It was a good message, right for the time, and Mike was buzzing afterwards. He thought it was one of the best songs he'd heard. "All you need is love. Love is all you need." Such a simple melody. And we all sang along. Later, Lennon invited Mike down to his gaff in Ascot and they socialised at some parties, but Mike always remained in awe of the Beatle. More a fan than a peer. He'd have swapped anything to be a Beatle rather than a Monkee.

Mike had just got himself a big place in Los Angeles, but it came with a bunch of sycophants. He wanted rid of them. When we were out, he'd keep ragging me: "I can't get on with my life with these guys around. I need someone like you to move them on. Come to America." I said, "I'm married. I've got kids. How can I?" I also thought, Throw them out yourself. But Mike kept on at me about these hangers-on, so I made out I'd got some big debts, one and a half grand's worth. That should have blown him off. It didn't. Mike wrote out the cheque and also sent a round-trip ticket. I landed in LA. £1,500 up front and with a holiday visa for three months. I ended up staying three years.

Looking back, the move wasn't the best decision for my marriage – Martin was only a baby – but everyone wants to go to America, right? The idea was to check it out and send for Margaret when I got myself a green card. Mike's lawyers were working on that as soon as I touched down. And then there I was on another sunny day in LA, 13 September 1967. A car screamed around the corner and out stepped one of The Monkees, all six foot five of him. Mike said, "You wanna drive?" I said, "You drive. It's your town." He said, "It's yours now, Alf." We drove back to town and Mike dropped me off at a rented apartment on Sunset Boulevard. He peeled off a few hundred bucks and tossed me the keys to my own car.

This was the time to be in California. New York had been hot a few years earlier, but now the West Coast was rocking. The Doors, Iggy And The Stooges and The Beach Boys were running all around town, and by 1969 Led Zeppelin would drop by on a regular basis to play Los Angeles in their attempt to break America. And right across the street from my place on Sunset was the legendary Whiskey A Go Go. Every band worth seeing made the pilgrimage to the Whiskey. It was a dark, no-nonsense club, wall to wall with blonde, blue-eyed teenage girls. In hotpants. Go-go girls frugging in their cages. Oh, man, the girls! Booths where the rock stars held court. Brian Wilson. The Who's Keith Moon. It was like a film-set fantasy, a dream. The girls would do the watusi and then wander out onto the Strip flashing peace signs. They'd put beads around me, give me flowers. Everyone was on something. Grass, mostly, but also 'ludes, whizz, H, valium, coke and acid. I settled on reefer. It suited me. I was a smoker. Also, I knew how to roll a good joint. Three papers, a nice cone. I became the number one joint-roller at parties. You didn't need a roach clip with my joints. They liked that.

It was probably a good time to move to California. In England, the Stones had just been busted for drugs at Keith Richards' country house and cops were raiding all sorts of parties. It was getting heavy, and what for? A bit of weed. A couple of months before I left for America, The Beatles, their manager, Brian Epstein, and a bunch of other names of the time petitioned for a change in the cannabis laws. An ad in *The Times* – Monday 24 July 1967, check it out – called the law against marijuana "immoral in principle and unworkable in practice". Sure, but nothing was going to change. The government didn't care what a bunch of longhairs had to say. Coppers were still busting up clubs and parties for a few ounces of hash or a bag of grass.

There didn't seem to be the same level of hassle in LA. The drug scene was exploding across California, and it seemed the thing to do. In June, Jimi Hendrix burned his guitar live at the fairgrounds in Monterey, where only the squarest of squares weren't doing pot, purple haze or a couple of milligrams of STP.

The next couple of months I spent in the Whiskey. Just tip up, scotch on the rocks, dance a bit (I still had the old Sam And Dave moves), hit on a chick. Another scotch. I remember catching a shambolic performance by The Doors there one night, Jim Morrison in leather trousers and a foul mood. He had his back to the crowd most of the night, but it was still electric.

Mike gave me a fancy job title, assistant record producer, but I didn't produce any records. I was there to push people out of Mike's way, and my first job was to dump Mike's hangers-on. There were about six sleeping in the living room of his house up on Mulholland Drive, in the Hollywood Hills, old friends from Texas. But Mike had got a young kid by now, Christian, and his wife, Phyllis, was fed up with them. Out they went.

Then Mike fixed me up with a house in Van Nuys, up above north Hollywood, in the Valley. San Fernando Valley. It was a shame to move off the Strip, but I needed something bigger because, after about six months, I sent for my wife and kids. I missed the kids, and the chicks down the Whiskey would have to go. Shame.

Now I had a problem. It would be easier to process the paperwork if I vouched for the family and fetched them from England, but I couldn't leave the US because I was still on a three-month tourist visa and illegal. Mike and I hatched a plan, Operation Monkee, planned like a raid from my Mau Mau days: Margaret and the boys fly to Ottawa; I fly to New York; Margaret takes the train to the Canadian border; I get up to Buffalo and check into a motor lodge; Margaret gets to the nearest border crossing, just down from Niagara Falls; I hire a car and driver; they cross the border; we all fly back to LA.

I remember it was snowing when we got there. And it was cold. Like a scene out of a spy movie. I sent the driver and the car over the border while I watched nervously from the US side. I was tense as hell, jumping up and down to keep warm.

Suddenly I saw Margaret and the boys. They were waved into an immigration office. Nothing to worry about. Minutes ticked by. What were they doing? Stick to the story. We're just on holiday. No, we don't know anyone in the US. We're staying at a hotel. Here's the address. The hired driver turned the engine off. Another ten minutes ticked by. Jesus, they've blown it, I thought. Then they were out the office and in the car. It turned back to cross into the US and Operation Monkee was a success. Life was going to be sweet. I was an assistant record producer who didn't need to produce, we were in southern California, the weather was great and The Monkees' TV show was a hit.

There was just one small problem: Mike Nesmith hated the TV series more than the fucking group. Absolutely loathed it. I'd drive Mike down to the studio on Mondays, Tuesdays and Wednesdays. He'd film from seven in the morning to about five or six, sometimes longer if they were out on location. He hated getting up in the morning to record that TV series, and on the way down Laurel Canyon he would bitch about the scripts for the show: "I fucking hate it. It's a stupid, dumb show." The Monkees. Moaners, more like.

And if the scripts didn't set him off, the schedule would. There was always something he could rail against. Rafelson and Schneider's company, Screen Gems, had their production office at the studio where the series was filmed and were always knocking around. Jack Nicholson was also down on set a lot, trying to break into acting, kidding around with Bob, but his career was going nowhere fast. This was way before *Easy Rider* and *Five Easy Pieces*. Nicholson wasn't much more than an office boy at the time, and we hung out together on the set to pass the time. He was funny, very funny, and with that same smile. We had a blast taking the piss out of The Monkees and clowning around behind the cameras.

Jack loved his draw. "Want a reefer, Jack?" "Is the Pope Catholic?" He was just a young kid, a good-looking guy, but a nobody, and there were always lots of good-looking guys around. What Jack got was an angle. He worked on cultivating his charm and catching tips off people like Schneider – who was a real networker – or Mickey Dolenz. It worked. Girls were always buzzing around Nicholson. We went down the Whiskey – where else? – a few times, and it was like watching a pro. A smile – that smile – a bit of chat and *bang*, he'd be in. He didn't need to become a movie star to get women. They loved him already. Lucky guy. Years later, I was working at a film festival in England and Nicholson was the number one player in Hollywood. He came over: "Hey, Alf, you fucking little Monkee. Got any draw?"

Nicholson was always hanging around with The Monkees and he'd often come up to Mike's house. I think this is where he got the idea to write *Head*. It was the last thing Mike needed, another Monkee vehicle, but it got Jack into writing with Rafelson and his first big break. The film was junk, just a bunch of nonsense scenes intercut with a few songs: 'Circle Sky', 'Daddy's Song', 'Can You Dig It'. Mickey, Peter, Davy and Mike in the war. Mickey, Peter, Davy and Mike boxing. Now, boxing was my thing, and that really was rubbish, although I did get to meet with the heavyweight champ Sonny Liston. He was an extra, with Frank Zappa and Vic Mature. Of course, *Head* is now a cult classic. It may have been good timing that The Monkees were over by the time Rafelson did his next film, *Five Easy Pieces*. With Nicholson – not Mickey, Peter, Davy and Mike – in the lead, the pair produced a real classic.

L-r: Martin Weaver, Jonathan Nesmith and Laurence Weaver in Mike Nesmith's dune buggy, near Palm Springs

Alf's son Laurence (left) with Jonathan Nesmith at Mike Nesmith's house in Los Angeles, wearing Alf's old boxing gloves

Alf with Mike Nesmith's white Eldorado at the Van Nuys house in Los Angeles

Alf's wife, Margaret, in the desert near Palm Springs

Alf's house in Van Nuys, Los Angeles, 1967

The next couple of years were good. I fell into the LA life. There was always something to do out at Mike's place, with him, Phyllis or the kids, but it wasn't onerous. Far from it. I wasn't really minding anyone. Then, sometime in 1968, the 'Born Free' lyricist, Don Black, phoned me from England. "I'm coming over with Tom Jones. Will you be around?" At the time, Jones The Voice wasn't well known in the States, and he'd just signed on to do a series of shows in Las Vegas to get his profile up. I picked Don and Tom up from the airport and we hit the Strip. As I said, Tom wasn't an unknown, but he was far from a household name. But that didn't stop the women. They were all over him. We'd sit at a table and the girls would come over and start hitting on Tom. Not me or Don. Tom. A real ladies' man. I guess guys like him and Nicholson have just got it. I think he disappeared with a lady or two on that tour.

Jones was also one of the biggest drinkers I've ever been with. At one after-show party, we stood at the bar and Tom must have knocked back ten pints, one after the other. *Wham.* He slammed the last empty glass on the bar and – "Cheerio, Alf" – walked out looking as if he'd never had a drop. A good Welsh lad from the valleys. It must be in their blood.

I used to spend a lot of time up at Mike's house shooting pool or mucking around with his sons, Christian and Jonathan. Mike would always be tinkering. As I said, country was his big thing, so it was only natural that Johnny Cash would drop by the house for impromptu jamming sessions, and he and Mike would sit in the studio for hours. Mike always had a guitar in his hand, and he was always writing songs. He'd sit around the house and I'd watch him construct his songs, take them off somewhere from just a few bars. Sometimes Mike would be stuck on a word. "What do you think, Alf? Got any good lines?" I'd toss in a couple of suggestions – ad libs, really – and he'd scribble something down. "I'll put your name on this one," he'd say, but of course I'd say, "No, it's only a few words." Sometimes I wish I hadn't been so quick to refuse a songwriting credit, because I remember looking through Mike's royalty statements. He was pulling down huge amounts of cash.

Around this time, we also got a call from Mike's producer, Tim Hardin. Tim had also worked with Elvis Presley and had got tickets to see the King in Las Vegas. This was a blast. Me, Mike, Phyllis, Margaret and her friend Ann. Vegas was unbelievable: the Strip at 3am, lit up like daylight; the air off the desert – hot, like a hairdryer. The Elvis show was a big deal, part of

Presley's big comeback, and he was pulling out all the stops: 'Heartbreak Hotel' to a kung-fu kick; 'Love Me Tender' sung to a young girl in the audience. He also looked great – pair of black-leather trousers, hair slicked back. He hadn't gone to seed at this point. 'Suspicious Minds'.

I can't remember how many nights he played, but a little party was thrown for him the night we were in town, upstairs at one of the Strip hotels. Tim took us up in an elevator. The doors slid open and there was the King working the room. He'd got real presence. Tim did the intros and we had a little chat. I said I'd help him out if he ever came to perform in the UK. "That sounds great, Alf." Of course, he never did. He also wanted to know everything about The Beatles. I caught Elvis a few years later, in New York, but the magic had already started to fade.

The Monkees all lived close to each other in LA. Mike was quite the family man by now. He was no hardcore rocker, although he was always the first Monkee to have the new Beatles albums, and the others would drive over to hear him play them. He'd play them over and over again. *Sgt Pepper's Lonely Hearts Club Band*, out at the beginning of June, was a favourite at Mike's playing parties. Then, in November 1968, came *The White Album*, as everyone called it. Mike and the rest of The Monkees were blown away by tunes like 'Back In The USSR' and 'Revolution 9'.

Mickey was nearby, on Laurel Canyon. He was the Monkee who always threw the parties. Loads of girls, lots of drink, all the bedrooms in use and me rolling the joints. Mickey had his wedding up at the Laurel Canyon house, out in the huge garden. A big marquee was erected by the pool and the cream of the LA rockocracy were there: Crosby, Stills, Nash And Young were there: "All right, Graham?" (I knew Graham Nash from The Hollies.) "Hi, Jack." Grinning Nicholson again. Everyone was smoking weed. Most of the guests were out of it and couldn't roll a joint to save their lives. I'd say, "Give it here. I'll do it." Three papers. Nice cone. Perfect.

Mike used to love driving. And riding bikes. He'd blast around LA on a Triumph, up and down Hollywood. Scared the shit out of anyone stepping off the sidewalk. Mike also had a place up near Palm Springs. He'd leave the Caddy in the garage for this trip and we'd shoot up there in his E-Type Jag. He could do 150mph easy in that. You could break records on the roads out there because they were so straight and flat. The needle would creep up and Mike would be whooping in the driving seat. Most of the time, I was fucking terrified.

The American Wichita Company

```
15221 ANTELO PLACE,
LOS ANGELES,
CALIFORNIA 90024,
U.S.A.


DEAR SIRS:


RE: REFERENCE OF MR WEAVER.

MR WEAVER WAS IN MY EMPLOYMENT FOR OVER THREE YEARS

AS ASSISTANT RECORD PRODUCER, HAVING MANY RESPONSIBILITIES
WHICH HE CARRIED OUT WITH THE GREATEST DISPATCH AND

ABILITY. HE WAS A MOST FAITHFUL AND LOYAL PART OF THIS
COMPANY AND I WOULD RECCOMMEND HIM MOST HEARTILY FOR

ANY CONSIDERATION.



SINCERLY

ROBERT M NESMITH
PRESIDENT.


rmn/os
```

Mike Nesmith's reference for Alf

Apart from speed, Mike's other obsession was guns. I thought that was an odd one, but I guess he was from Texas. The frontier spirit. Hunting, shooting and fishing. Mike had all his guns racked up in a cabinet in the house – rifles, revolvers, pistols. The whole nine yards. One time, we were hanging out at his house, playing pool, when Mike fetched out a .38 automatic. "We're going downtown, Alf. I want you to carry this." Sure. OK. It was heavy but easier to handle than the British-army-issue revolvers out in Africa. Little Richard had asked Mike downtown to watch him play in a club around Alameda Street, some dive in some back street. It reminded me of the time I took Otis Redding to Brixton a few years before. And there weren't too many white folks down at this gig. In fact, there weren't any. That was probably what spooked Mike out, and why I had a gun in the waistband of my trousers. But there wasn't any trouble. Everyone was too hooked on the music or the good grass being passed around. That was good news. I didn't want to shoot anyone.

I did shoot a bear, though. At least, I'm claiming it. This was Mike's idea. One day, he decided to get a party together and shoot a few caribou in Alaska. I was in. We got kitted out at an army-surplus store in LA. This'll be like Mount Kenya, I thought. Parka, boots, mittens. I've still got that jacket, and every time I wear it – usually to walk the dogs in winter – I'm reminded of that trip. We caught a flight up to Anchorage and then chartered a private plane out to an island a couple of hundred miles away. We holed up for about a week in a couple of log cabins. Just the essentials. Us against the elements. I was a city boy and lost without the local supermarket, but Mike thought he was the last of the great white hunters.

We had to catch dinner. I remember freezing my ass off for hours waiting for the fish to bite through holes we punched in the ice. And then we'd tramp for miles across the crisp white snow in search of the big game. *Crunch, crunch, crunch.* Most days drew a blank, and we'd head back to the cabins to polish off a bottle of bourbon and thaw out in front of a fire. However, on the last day, after another few hours of trudging through snow, I spotted a bear. It was a few hundred yards away. I inched closer, rifle in hand. I aimed the rifle. *Crack!* The bear immediately dropped. Dead. I hauled up to examine the kill and immediately felt sick. The bear's blood was leaking onto the virgin white snow. I could only hear the sound of the wind and my breathing. It was one of the saddest sights I've seen in my life.

One day, back in LA, we were sitting around the pool at Mike's place.

Alf with his governor, Mike Nesmith, at a recording session in 1969

Alf at A&M Studios, Los Angeles, 1967. The caption reads, "Sleeping beauty got the white socks"

Alf at the opening of his club in Los Angeles

The drinks were coming out cold that day, and strong. Mike didn't skimp on the measures. Now, this pool was really something. It started off inside the house, snaked under a glass wall – one side of the house, I guess – and outside into Mike's back yard. That's where we were. You could dive in, swim right under that glass and come up by the bar in the lounge, fix a Martini – gin Martini, with a twist – and swim right out of there again.

As I said, we're lounging around and shooting the breeze. The kids are mucking around somewhere. Then one of Martin's friends comes running up crying. "Martin's in the pool!" What? "Martin's fallen in!" Shit. I ran into the house and there was Martin, floating face-down. Oh, Christ! Arms out. Lifeless, or so it seemed. I dived straight in and pulled him out. Someone rang the medics while I worked on Martin, trying to get him breathing again, pumping his chest, giving my son the kiss of life. Martin spluttered back to life and I sat back, drained. That was close.

The ambulance had arrived by now and the medics pushed forward. "What's happened here?" I told them. "And have you got medical insurance, sir?" I got the guy by his neck. "My son has almost fucking drowned. I don't give a shit whether I've got medical insurance. Just get him into hospital." They did.

I don't know if this was the last straw with Margaret. Obviously, she was upset. Who wasn't? But things seemed to go on the slide from here on in. Margaret was getting homesick. She'd been 18 months away from her family. And didn't I know! I got told every day. One problem was that she didn't drive – lethal, in LA – so she was stuck back at the house in Van Nuys, trapped. Christmas came and she decided to return home for the holidays with the boys. I couldn't go with her because of my visa problems, and I waved goodbye at the airport. "See you in a couple of weeks."

Two weeks later, I got a letter, not my wife and kids. It went something like, "Dear Alf. I am not coming back..." Diabolical. I wrote and phoned her, but Margaret wouldn't change her mind. I couldn't understand it. We were six miles from Santa Monica beach. The sun shone nearly every day. I had a decent job and we had everything that we could ask for, not a crummy house in south London. I loved the life. But I was on my own again.

I spent more time up at Mike's house. He didn't have a secretary and liked me to answer the phone in a plummy English accent. "Good morning. Mike Nesmith's residence. How can I help you?" He loved that.

I went on a few US tours with Mike, and once up to San Francisco to watch them play the Cow Palace, but quite often I stayed behind to look after Phyllis and the kids. When Mike was away like this, I had a lot of time on my hands. To kill it, I opened a club and started an affair.

I opened the club out in the valley. It had a great little stage and a small bar, well stocked. A nice drinking den. We had a great opening night because Mike and the rest of The Monkees came down to party. For a while, I swapped the Whiskey for my club, the Place. We had a few celebs drop by, but it was busted up by the cops within six months. Don't ask me why.

Then, one night, I met a Jewish girl. Michelle. We were like chalk and cheese – she was very polished, I was a bit of rough. Her old man owned some kind of orange-juice franchise and was minted. Mine spent his last pennies on booze. But somehow we got along fine. We hung out a lot together, went to concerts, to the beach at Santa Monica and Venice. I remember Jerry Lee Lewis invited Mike and me to a club one night and I took Michelle along. I was in love, I guess. However, I had a problem: just before meeting Michelle, I told Mike I'd have to go back to England and rescue my marriage. I missed Laurence and Martin. I said I'd stay a few months to sort out a few loose ends. Things were coming apart with The Monkees, anyway. Mike was desperate to leave. I remember trying to persuade him to hang on. "Stay another year. Maybe two. By then you'll be set, financially." But he wouldn't have it. He wanted out. I remember the morning he called a meeting to end it all. He was pretty quiet on the drive down to the studio to meet the others. I stayed out in the car and Mike was in and out before The Byrds had finished singing 'Mr Tambourine Man' on the car radio. That was it, the end of The Monkees. In less than five minutes.

The thing with Michelle tore us both up. When I told her I was returning to London, we were both in tears. I loved her, and we probably should have married. I never saw her again. But it was the right time to leave Los Angeles. A few months later, in August, and just around the corner from Mike's place, Charlie Manson – the man who had hoped to become a Monkee – ordered the killing of Sharon Tate, up in the Hollywood Hills.

6 Fab Four

I worked for Brian Epstein for just one week. It was the last week of The Beatles' manager's life. Now here I was, back in Britain and bumming around, living off the Walworth Road again, with the family. Margaret's premature departure and the affair with Michelle had put a strain on our marriage. We stuck at it for the sake of the kids, but it was effectively over. I wanted – needed – a job, something to throw myself into. Certainly not nine to five. I couldn't do that.

I was kicking my heels. I decided to visit my brother at his flower shop in Shepherds Market. There I was chatting to Dennis – "Jesus, life can be dull, sometimes" – and I clock Peter Brown waltzing along Curzon Street. Brown was one of The Beatles' inner circle, a funny-looking bloke and, in Brian's day, second in command. He was a mate of Epstein's from their Liverpool days. Very smart. I knew him from the Artist Car Services days. I'd done a few jobs for The Beatles in '65, '66 and early '67.

Wednesday 1 March 1967   Beatles recording at Abbey Road

Just messages and a bit of driving. Not too much strongarm stuff. I called after Brown.

"Awright, Alf. What you been doing?"

I tell him about the job with Mike Nesmith.

"Yeah, The Monkees. In LA. Great. What you doing now?" he asks.

"Right now, Pete, looking for a job." Don Murfet's mob were still in Camden. Moved to Camden Road, bigger premises. Don had thrown me a few jobs since I had got back from the States, but nothing permanent.

"Well, listen, Alf. Apple needs a good man with your sort of experience. Get yourself down to Savile Row."

I had mixed feelings. Epstein's death had been a big fucking downer. The Beatles hadn't toured for years, and now I was thinking of going to work for them. But nothing else was in the frame. "Yeah, I guess. Where are they now?" Brown gave me the address of Apple HQ at 3 Savile Row and I wandered the few blocks east to sign on. During the ten-minute walk, I thought about the last time I saw Brian Epstein.

It was mid August 1967 and Apple rang Artist Car Services. Brian's man had gone on holiday. Could I look after him for a bit? This meant a bit of driving. No problem. It was going to be an easy little job before I blew off to California with Mike Nesmith in September.

I got myself down to Chapel Street, off Belgrave Square. Number 24. Nice place. Epstein was a quiet sort of guy. I knew he was a pillhead and a poof, but he was always immaculately dressed and calm. No real hint of a Scouse accent. We went out to a big garage, where he kept a Bentley. We were going to drive that. OK. Epstein said he was planning a trip to the US in a couple of weeks' time and he wanted some new duds, so we spent most of the week in and out of shops on Jermyn Street. Herbie Frogg. Turnbull & Asser. Nice schmutter. Sometimes I'd turn up in the morning and sit around reading the paper while he ponced himself up ready to meet the day. Then Jermyn Street again. More shops. He'd come back loaded down with bags.

He also went to EMI – then in Manchester Square – for good reason. Epstein had a car phone and I could hear him trying to renegotiate The Beatles' contract with the label. He was saying it wasn't good enough. Maybe that was a pressure. His own contract was also due for renegotiation in September. Maybe that was more pressure, but he didn't show it. Then there were a few parties. I knew he was a bit of Brighton, so he probably fixed himself up with a couple of rents. It didn't bother me. Live and let live.

Later on in the week, he said he was off to his place near Uckfield, in Sussex. Kingsley Hall. Could I drive him down? But later, he decided to drive himself. It was the bank-holiday weekend. "Have a great weekend, Alf. I'll see you Tuesday or give you a ring." That was it. There never was another week's work. Epstein apparently tired of Sussex and drove back to London on the Saturday. He took six sleeping pills that night. Drink and pills don't mix. The inquest said accidental overdose, but there were wild rumours that he committed suicide or had been murdered. I think the coroner got it right. It was an accident, not a deliberate death.

The first I heard was on the evening news. Fucking hell. I was sitting with Margaret, and the first thing I thought was, That's another week's work gone. Then I felt a bit guilty. Maybe I could have done something else for him. What would have happened if I'd insisted on driving him down to Sussex? Should I have called over the weekend? The Beatles had been down in Wales meeting with the Maharishi and were telephoned. Later, when they knew I'd been with Brian that week, they asked whether I thought he'd killed himself. I said no. That seemed to help them, but Brian's death changed a lot with The Beatles. After that, the atmosphere was heavier. Everyone was down. It was dreadful. He'd been a pal, the fifth Beatle. Maybe there wouldn't have been any Beatles without him.

I got the Apple job. Titles weren't a big part of the Apple organisation, but I was head of security, bodyguard and chauffeur all rolled into one. On £1,765 per annum. Payable weekly. Normal hours of work between 10am and 6pm. Yeah, sure. It was good to be back working with The Beatles.

Another thing not on the job description but part of the job: sign the autographs. I did this for most of the people I ever worked with. Some were tricky to get a handle on, like Paul's, but I'd practise at night, at home, in front of the telly. I'd soon get them down pretty good. George's and Ringo's were pretty easy and, instead of disappointing the fans who turned up at Apple, we'd have a ready-made supply, or I'd nip out back and squiggle a bit. It was better than saying, "The Beatles are too busy." They were happy for me to do that, and the fans went away happy. I probably did a better John Lennon signature than John Lennon. I took care over them. But I wonder about those memorabilia auctions. Some of those signed pictures. I wonder how many had been signed by me?

As I said, I knew the boys from three or four years ago and had introduced Mike Nesmith to John at the 'All You Need Is Love' sessions. They'd had a few office boys back then. They did the weekly shop for The Beatles' wives. Can you imagine that? Lennon's list: cornflakes, pound of mince, fruit and veg. That kind of thing. The Harrisons' list: tea, biscuits, choccies. They never went for anything too fancy. None of The Beatles were into three-star Michelin cooking in the '60s. This was plain-old Scouser grub. Chips with everything. Omelettes were a favourite. Lots of tea – tea you could stand a spoon up in. George liked his Earl Grey. Egg soldiers. Oh, yeah, and John loved his butties – jam butties and a mug of tea. Lovely.

Maureen Cox, Ringo Starr, Patti Boyd and George Harrison arrive at Heathrow Airport

The Beatles' Mercedes and the Apple drivers. (Alf second right)

Sometimes I'd deliver the weekly groceries to The Beatles' houses. John, Ringo and George all lived near each other at the time – John at Kenwood, down near Weybridge; Ringo near him, in Sunny Heights; and George at Kinfauns, in Esher. Cynthia Lennon, Maureen Cox, Patti Boyd. Cynthia was very homely. No pretence about her. Her and John were just like a wealthy suburban couple, out in a big mock-Tudor house with a few acres. Right next to a golf course. Perfect for John. Sometimes he'd be at the piano and Julian – who was very young at this stage – would crawl around. But you had to be wary with John. You never knew what sort of mood he'd be in. Sometimes sweet, sometimes a fucking maniac.

One time, Brown handed me a package. It wasn't groceries. "What's this?"
"Fuck knows."

Fine. When I got down to the house, John was upstairs, waiting. And chatting to a bloke I'd only seen in the papers. Maybe in *The International Times*, the blueprint for the revolution. That was always lying around at Apple. Who was it? Black guy. Beard. Striking. Michael de Freitas. The black power activist Michael de Freitas Abdul Malik. Michael X to his friends. Mike. Mickey X. He was always being profiled in the underground press. X was doing for black militancy in Britain what the American civil-rights leader Malcolm X had tried in the States.

And John was helping him. This was John's thing. That was what he was into. Militancy. Revolution. Stirring things up. Or so he wanted us to believe. Black consciousness was going to get a kick start somewhere, I suppose, but a big fucking house in Ascot with a white Roller outside seemed a strange place for a couple of so-called radicals.

Standing in that bedroom, they looked a strange pair: John slim, late 20s, bearded; Michael X the same but black. Black and white brothers. John would have loved that.

"Here it is. Thanks, Alf." John snatched at the pack and opened the envelope. Full of cash. Damn! Seven grand spilled out onto the bed. I know because John counted it out: "Fifty, one hundred, one fifty, two, two fifty, three…" It took a few minutes. Michael X and I stood there counting along. "Three fifty, four…" I doubt either of us had seen so much cash before. I know I hadn't. Me a working-class kid from Camden; X from Trinidad and into pimping and blues clubs since arriving in Notting Hill.

"Six thousand nine hundred, six nine fifty, seven thousand moolah. Great. It's all there."

What did Lennon think? I was going to help myself? Although, in the '60s, that would have set me and Margaret up nicely. John bundled up the £50 bills and handed them over to Mr X. When the Notting Hill riots kicked off in the '50s, the Black Power leader had made a name for himself by calling on the brothers to arm themselves against the racist gangs. "Get some iron." Now he'd got real power, seven grand's worth, and the support of a Beatle. John's cash was going to help him open his Black House project, but I wondered what British black activists would think if they knew a white hippy was giving them hand-outs. John was always one to give a lot of money away. CND, the anti-apartheid movement – he helped them all. And £7,000 was no big deal for him. Small change. After all, he was a working-class hero.

Ringo and Maureen had got married in 1965 and seemed very happy. Ringo was always larking around, sometimes out in the garden in his trunks. Sunbathing Ringo. George was getting into the Hare Krishna thing, around then. He married Patti in January 1966 and they were always lovey-dovey. Patti was a beautiful woman. For me, George was the best Beatle. I'd do a lot for him. I remember when he moved to Friar Park, in Henley, a few years later. I used to go down to help him clear the grounds of that place. There were carvings all over the place, inside and out. It was as if the place had been built with George in mind.

Then, one night, he crashed his car. This was in the early '70s. George had been driving to see Ricky Nelson in concert at the Royal Albert Hall, but England was in the middle of a black-out. No street lights. Can you believe it? The country was in the grip of the unions and power was being rationed. So up comes George and Patti in the old Merc. *Wham.* Straight into a roundabout. The Merc was a mess – it was a write-off – but fortunately George and Patti were OK.

A day or so later, George rings up. "Alf, they moved the roundabout." That was his little joke. But I think he was a little worried, being a guitarist, because his back and shoulder were giving him some grief. "My back's killing me. It's really sore if I play for too long." Christ, what was I going to do? Then I remembered the physio at my beloved Arsenal, Fred Street. He could work wonders on the players. Maybe he could help with a Beatle. I called up and Fred was only to happy to get his healing hands on George Harrison. We went down to Highbury about four or five times. George got a massage session while I wandered around looking at the trophies.

George was always up for a chat. Asked how you were, that was George. But Lennon and Paul could be a bit removed. Cool. I didn't have as many dealings with McCartney, but he was always slightly aloof.

In 1965, Paul had moved into a house in Cavendish Avenue, near the cricket ground, Lords. But Paul never offered me a cup of tea. Sometimes made me stand around outside like a spare prick. In fact, I can't ever remember him inviting me into his gaff. Maybe thought I'd tread dirt into his carpet. But it was always business with Paul. No fun. He'd been seeing Jane Asher for years. In December 1967, just after I'd flown out to America, Paul and Jane got engaged. Before Paul moved to St John's Wood, they'd lived together with Jane's family in Wimpole Street. I'd sometimes take him down to these private airports out near Luton, or in Surrey, for him to fly off in a tiny prop plane to meet her somewhere. Sometimes she'd fly in and we'd be there waiting to meet her. It was like a scene from *Casablanca*, two young lovers at the airport. But it was all over between them by August 1968.

Paul always seemed very quiet, sitting in the back of the car. Always writing, working up a song. Very focused. Same as when they were recording – McCartney was always the bossy one. Sometimes I'd go down to the recording sessions at Abbey Road, not far from Paul's house. They did everything at Abbey in those days. In 1965, *Rubber Soul*. Then *Revolver*, 1966. Always Studio One, the big studio, and always with producer George Martin.

Mal Evans would be there, a big brute and a Beatle roadie. Mal was shot by LA police a few years later. That was a shame. Another link with The Beatles from the very early days. He got pretty down after The Beatles split and got hopped up on drugs one night in January 1976. The cops were called. Mal somehow got hold of a rifle and was shot.

Neil Aspinall would be there most nights, too. Neil was an old mate of the first Beatles drummer, Pete Best, and the group's former driver. Now heading up Apple. I would sit around the desk with Martin and a couple of engineers, just watching and listening. Mal and Neil would be in the studio with the band, setting up or moving equipment. The Beatles always recorded at night, then, because there were less press around to bother them. They'd start at seven and work through to the early morning. Ringo used to sit there and would never say a word. Nothing. No joking, no looning around. Just sat at his kit. I sometimes wondered why they'd ditched Best for Ringo. OK, I'm no musician, but after hearing Buddy Rich and a couple of other sticksmen, Ringo didn't seem that special.

George didn't say anything, either. George had to wait a couple of years before he could get his stuff recorded, because John and Paul were the only Beatles songwriters on these albums. Later, George used to get a bit cut up about this, especially during the Abbey Road recordings, thought he should be getting a bit more out, and would bitch about Paul not listening or taking his contributions seriously. "What do you think? Could you use it just to fill up the album, if you haven't got anything?" That was strange. He'd known these guys for years and yet seemed embarrassed to show his songs off.

John was John, sometimes moody in the studio, sometimes chatty. He could have a good sense of humour. Like, in his Mercedes, he had a loudspeaker installed so he could shout at pedestrians – "Get out of the fookin' way!" – and they got out of the way. But it was always apparent that he was in control. He'd usually listen to what George had to say. More so than Paul, anyway.

It was McCartney who always seemed to have the most input. On those records, at least. Lennon and McCartney rarely wrote together. John wrote his songs, and the stuff he wrote he sang. The same with Paul. It wasn't ever really Lennon and McCartney. Then George might pipe up with a riff. "Listen to this." They would all stop and listen while George strummed a few chords. There was never much laughter in those sessions. Sometimes the atmosphere would definitely be strained and they'd take hours to do things, with Paul offering new direction. They would play the same bits over and over and over again. 'Drive My Car' – they'd change something and then do it again. They used to go over and over stuff, play the same old chords over and over again, just to get it right. Over and over. 'Drive My Car'. It was incredibly boring to watch – 'Drive My Car' – although I did feel privileged. This was history in the making. Then, at three in the morning, "Come on, lads. Let's go down the Ad Lib." That was Paul again. Or they'd say, "Let's have a break. It's not happening." The next day, it would be the same. This time, Paul's song 'Eleanor Rigby', again and again and again.

But I was glad to be back at Apple, and on 30 January 1969 that was the place to be, at Savile Row. Better still, on the roof. The Beatles were playing up there that day. Again, history was being made, but this time the whole world was invited to watch. The last public performance by the world's best pop group. And I was there.

It had caught me a bit by surprise. The Beatles had released *The White Album* in November and were already working on a new album at Twickenham Studios, which was being filmed for a documentary, *Let It Be*. But from what I saw of the group that January, things weren't going too well. Ringo had already pulled a big tantrum and George had temporarily left The Beatles. He'd been pissed that Paul was pulling rank in the studio, by all accounts. They were both now back in the fold, but they all looked fucking miserable. A gig on the roof of Apple was, therefore, the last thing I expected. I guess it was easier to do a concert a few flights up rather than at the Roundhouse or the Palladium. Also, I wouldn't have missed it for the world.

That morning, we all gathered at the offices – Brown; George Martin, the producer, working with the boys downstairs; Derek Taylor, the press guy; the receptionist, Debbie; Mal Evans. Who else was there? Oh yeah, Jimmy Clark. Me and Jimmy were in charge of the door. Keep the riff-raff out. "Mornin', Ringo. Nice jacket." We let him in. The rest of The Beatles were there by midmorning. We had already started to set things up on the roof. Apple didn't have a lift, and I remember lugging all the heavy equipment upstairs. I don't remember Neil Aspinall being around that day. It was a pretty basic set-up, a few amps. Basic kit for Ringo. It was also pretty fucking cold up there, and John and George wrapped up in big fur coats.

Then they started playing and recording. Amazing! 'Get Back'. 'Let It Be'. Great. Almost immediately, the office windows opposite were full of faces peering over. Some City-gent types in their pinstripes, secretaries in Mary Quant. Some even made it up onto the roofs nearby. Everyone wanted to get a view and not much work got done that day. Then a buzz went around London and crowds poured into the surrounding narrow streets. They couldn't see much, but they could hear The Beatles. There were people everywhere and the traffic on Savile Row soon ground to a halt. Regent Street, around the corner, was totally blocked. Everyone was straining to get a view, but I had the best one. I was up on the roof, watching everything. But of course there were always some fans and photographers trying to get in, and me and Jimmy occasionally ran down to slam the door in someone's face.

There were always fans hanging around Apple, asking to speak to Ringo or George. Everyone asked for Ringo. They probably thought he was the most approachable Beatle. They knew what they'd get with John: "Go on, fuck off."

Some of the Apple Scruffs were there, too, as usual. These were a handful of kids who hung around Apple, Abbey Road and EMI, in Manchester Square, basically anywhere where The Beatles were. George had his girls – Carol, Cathy, Lucy. Paul had his – Margo, Jill. They were always hassling for autographs and taking pictures. Probably the most loyal fans in the world. They'd wait, rain or shine, for a Beatle to appear. Sometimes they never did.

It was turning into a siege at the offices, that day. No one could leave and no one was getting in. Then the cops were called. There was a police station further down on Savile Row. One copper says, "There are people all over the street. You have to stop this noise."

We weren't having any of it. "It's not our fault people are all over the street," said Jim. "It's your job to clear them."

The Beatles were also into getting nicked. It would have made good theatre for the film to be dragged off the roof by the law. They weren't stopping for anything. Besides, they were really cooking. As they played, they got more into it. 'Across The Universe'. They were genuinely excited when it was all over, especially McCartney – he was on a real high. I think they enjoyed playing live again. Remember, they hadn't done that for years. But they were a good band. There was some talk about doing other one-offs, but they never came off.

Those half-dozen tunes up on the roof was about the last time I saw all The Beatles together. 'Come Together'. Things had been changing at Apple over the last few months. With Brian gone, The Beatles had been without a manager for years. They'd created Apple Corps Ltd in 1967 to organise their affairs, but it was leaking money all over the place and they hadn't got anyone to plug the holes. John, Paul, George and Ringo were trying to sort out who that should be.

On 3 February, a few days after their rooftop concert, they signed up Allen Klein. Klein was an American and an accountant. He'd been around the block and sailed pretty close to the wind. He'd already fallen out with The Rolling Stones by the time he tipped up with The Beatles, and within a few years his company, Abkco – named after his and wife Betty's initials – was being pressed by the Internal Revenue Service and New York's Department of Tax Collection.

Klein has had a lot of bad press, but I got on well with him. When he was in the country, he stayed at the Inn On The Park, the Dorchester or the

3 Savile Row London W.1.

Apple Corps postcard

Alf and Allen Klein

Intercontinental. He had the best relationship with John. It was Lennon who brought Klein in. We'd go down to John's house, sometimes to George's. Never Paul's.

As I said, John wanted him in. Ringo and George went along with John. Paul didn't. Paul had met Linda, Linda Eastman. Now he wanted her old man, Lee Eastman, a New York lawyer with his own practice, Eastman & Eastman, to handle The Beatles' affairs. Not Klein. But Paul was due to marry Linda in March, and John and the others didn't want their bandmate's father-in-law in charge of their finances. Around the office, everyone thought Paul was trying to pull a stroke, get a better deal. But then, we didn't know Klein.

There was a lot of paranoia at the time. Take the Christmas party. There was one every year, but there were two camps: the Apple people, who had been brought in by The Beatles, and the Abkco people, brought in by Klein and perceived as interlopers. Both sides stood at either side of the room, bitching about each other.

Despite the politics, Klein got the job, but Paul did manage to get Lee and his son, John, appointed as general counsel to Apple the day after Klein was hired. Paul said he wanted them to keep an eye on what Klein was up to. But after Klein came on board, McCartney made less use of his office at Apple. All the Beatles had one. Lennon's was the first office on the ground floor. Upstairs was a front office for all four of them. They'd meet here for the big pow-wows or for the Apple annual general meeting, like the one on 21 August that year. Then Klein, George, Ringo and Paul each had their separate offices. It was rare that they'd be in the building together.

My job during 1969 also now included keeping close to Klein, but he was only in the UK about one week in every eight. He was mostly based at his glass tower in New York, the Abkco offices, on Broadway. A bit later in the year, Allen asked me to pick up his new car. Actually, it was John's old car, his Rolls Royce Phantom V limousine. EUC 100C. Lennon had bought it in 1966 and completely resprayed it (white) and refitted its interior (white shag and white seats). John liked white. Lennon and Klein sealed the deal. $50,000, I think. Good price, John. I picked the car up at Hoopers in Kilburn and ended up driving it for the next decade, on and off.

The Beatles spluttered on. Paul wed Linda on 12 March in Marylebone. A week later, John made it legal with Yoko Ono in Gibraltar.

A lot has been written about Yoko, about her influence. Did she split up The Beatles? Was it Allen Klein? Or John or Paul? I don't know. I don't know if anyone really knows, although John did want to leave in late 1969. How much that was down to Yoko is just guesswork.

But I know one thing, because I saw it: she created tension. Lots of it. And strife. Most of the Apple staff resented her, and I never thought much of her. Always in the way. Even though a lot of people had been around longer than her, things had to be done her way or not at all. She always managed to wind people up, upset them. Maybe she was insecure and wanted to be boss, but she could have been open. She never was. I don't think I saw her smile. And there was always a new joke about Yoko going around the office. Not well thought of.

I also noticed that she had started to drop in on a lot of the recordings. Yoko would sit in the studio and talk to John. Whisper, really. A few words every few minutes. She'd never interrupt or criticise Paul, but she'd whisper to John and everyone could see that. As if she had the ear of the King. You could sometimes cut the air with a knife, and Paul would say, "There used to be four of us. Now there are five." Although never to Lennon's face. But what was anyone going to do? Yoko was going out with one of the biggest names in the pop world, and that gave her the power. Incredible, really.

I remember taking Phil Spector down to John's house at Tittenhurst Park, Ascot. Spector had been brought in to work on *Let It Be*, to stick a load of horns and pipes on it. Now, Phil Spector was pretty crazy, an absolute nutter, but Phil got on well with John. Lennon really respected him. Had him in to do 'Imagine'.

So there they are, Phil, John and Yoko. Three big egos in one room. I knew there'd be trouble, and sure enough something kicked off. John wanted Spector to play the piano on a track. "No." That's Yoko. Blimey, I thought. Why doesn't she stick with the art? If you could call it that. "No, John. You must play it." Yoko thinks John will make a better fist of it. It's just a piano part. And there's John saying, "I think Phil will be better." So we get into this big ding-dong about something that John and Spector could have sorted in seconds. But that's how it was with Yoko – never simple, never easy. What does she know about the piano?

Another time with Yoko – this was after John had been killed – I delivered something to her at a hotel in Knightsbridge. Can't remember the name of the place. Up I go. I knock on the door. I'm in, and there's four security guys in there. Big guys, all American, loping around and wanting to know who I am and what I fucking want. What I want? I'm doing the favour here. So I said, "You guys think you're pros? If you were doing this properly, you'd have at least two guys outside. No one should come in unless you know them. If I had a gun, I could have shot the lot of you." Then I remember thinking, What does Yoko need four minders for, anyway? The Beatles never had that many. Sometimes they got by with none.

The Beatles were in Abbey Road for most of August 1969, recording *Abbey Road*. Things seemed to be pretty normal. However, there were always whispers around the office that something was up, that it might be the last album, but there were always rumours about something. Twentieth of August was an historic date. We didn't know it at the time, but it was the last time the four Beatles recorded in the studio together.

From around September, the whispering campaign at Apple went into overdrive, but we never really got any information. I remember asking Klein what was going on, but he just stonewalled me. "Oh, nothing," he'd say. "Don't worry about a thing, Alf." I'm not sure The Beatles really knew where they stood then. John could change his mind on a

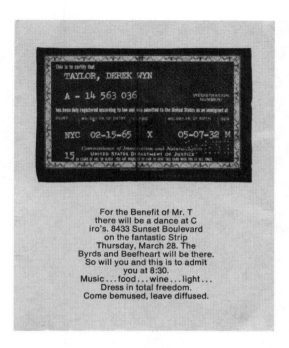

For the Benefit of Mr. T
there will be a dance at C
iro's. 8433 Sunset Boulevard
on the fantastic Strip
Thursday, March 28. The
Byrds and Beefheart will be there.
So will you and this is to admit
you at 8:30.
Music . . . food . . . wine . . . light . . .
Dress in total freedom.
Come bemused, leave diffused.

Invitation to Beatles publicity man
Derek Taylor's party

Beatles Christmas wrapping paper, featuring employees of Apple, including Alf

sixpence. Maybe he'd reconsider. And life did continue pretty much as normal at Apple. The Beatles still turned up, glum. Ringo and George would stick together more, now, and Paul made it clear he couldn't stand Allen. Paul's solo album *McCartney* was ready.

Then, one day in April 1970, the place went mad. I arrived at Apple around ten, as normal. A couple of The Beatles were already there, John and George. Paul had stopped coming in at this point, concentrating on his record. The place was buzzing. "What's going on?" I asked one of the secretaries.

"I think it's all over," she said.

I couldn't take it in to start with. "What is?" She looked at me. She was about to cry. "You mean The Beatles are breaking up?"

It sounds stupid. Although it was obvious the group had got problems, no one actually expected them to split. The Beatles can't do that! They're The Beatles! Fuck.

I guess it made sense. 1969 had been a strange time for them. A lot of raw anger from John; Paul missing recording sessions. It seems the final straw was John, Ringo and George attempting to stop Paul from releasing his album before *Let It Be* hit the shops. It would be bad business to have The Beatles versus Macca in the charts. As I heard it, Paul stuck to his guns. Told them to stick it. That didn't go down well with John and Allen.

McCartney then told the press that it was all over, as far as he was concerned. No future plans to record with The Beatles. Why should he? We heard later that, months before, John had already told the others that he wanted out of the group. He just hadn't told anyone else.

So that was it. At least no one had died. But I felt bad. I'd been with Apple just over a year. That was all I was going to get with The Beatles. I had a lot longer with Abkco, but that's not the same. The real end came at the end of the year, when Paul filed a suit demanding "the dissolution of The Beatles". Now, that really got everyone fired up, John, Ringo and George especially. They contested the suit, and it started to look like Paul was breaking up The Beatles. It took about a year to get to court. I don't remember much about that year. Like the phoney war. George started work on *All Things Must Pass* sometime in May, and I was pleased he was doing that. It was like he'd been given a new lease of life, with The Beatles on the ropes. It was sort of a depressing time, like life couldn't move on, and I also began to wonder if I should get out of the business.

Pages from the monthly book *Apple Scruff*, 1971

Just before The Beatles' court case, I thought I was bad for the minding business. Got myself a hex. The black spot, or some voodoo thing. The thing was, I'd worked with Brian Epstein and a week later he had wound up dead. Now, that's not good PR. Looks bad on the CV, that. No one wants a bodyguard on a death trip. Then, one week in September 1970, I met Jimi Hendrix. Eight days later, he was dead.

This is what happened. Mike Nesmith was back in London. "Alf, it's Mike. Want to earn a bundle?" Mike was Monkee-less. He'd split from the craziness of Mickey, Davy and Pete and was with his own band, The First National Band. That was a pretty ropey name for a group, but he'd had enough of wackiness. First National, now that sounded serious. They played his songs. "We're playing at the Roundhouse. Come up, do your stuff and then we'll have a party." Sounded like fun.

The gig in Camden Town was...well, it wasn't The Monkees. Four years earlier, Mike was being mobbed. Now the crowds were thinner, older, but Mike seemed happier. People were taking him seriously as a muso. One of them was Jimi Hendrix. Mike told me he'd toured with the guitarist on The Monkees' 1967 tour of the US. The Monkees and Hendrix – not a partnership made in heaven, but Mike was pretty in awe of Jimi. I think he wanted him involved because he was a serious musician, not a teenybopper.

Anyway, Mike says, "Let's have a party." Why not? I was always up for one. No work, parties, really. Everyone's too stoned or fucked up to cause any real trouble. Hendrix was in London and one of the first on the invite list. He turns up with the party in full swing. This is at the Inn On The Park, down Mayfair way, 10 September. I could see Hendrix was really out of it, in a pair of purple pants, long shirt, lots of detail, waistcoat. And he'd got a bird in tow. I don't know if he'd just pulled her. Maybe she was a regular fixture. He told us he was booked into the Cumberland Hotel, just up the road, at Marble Arch, but I think he was bunked up with a girlfriend someplace.

It was the first time I'd met Hendrix. He'd played at East Afton Farm – the Isle of Wight Festival – a few weeks before, but I'd missed that. I drove George Harrison down to catch the ferry at Southampton but didn't make the trip over the water myself. A pity, that, but I had also taken my boys down for the ride. I'll always regret not going. You always think there'll be plenty of time to catch up with things in life, but it doesn't always work out that way. I heard from George that Jimi had been great – 'Purple Haze', 'Voodoo Chile', 'Hey Joe' – but also that the whole thing had been a mess, security wise.

So I missed the Isle of Wight, but here was Jimi now – axe hero, King Guitar. Not with the Fender Stratocaster, strung left-handed, but in his party clothes. I was bowled over with how polite he was, even out of his head. Everything was please this, please that. Thank you very much. You're most kind. Me, Mike and Jimi chatted for a bit. Not easy. Jimi was all over the place. But then, so were most of us. There was a lot of Mandrax around at the time. He also talked so quietly, it was hard to pick up what he was saying. But he laughed a lot. He wasn't down.

So the party's swinging, some Beatles and Rolling Stones – 'Street Fighting Man'. Even played a bit of Hendrix. Mike liked his Hendrix. Then I saw Jimi again. This is a bit later. He was on his own. Odd, that. I thought rock stars always had an entourage. And his bird had gone missing. But there he was, standing in the middle of this ballroom, drink in hand. Bit of a loner, maybe. Liked his own space. I liked that. I might have had another word, just chit-chat. He wasn't too steady on his pins at this stage but still friendly, still polite as hell.

He comes over later. I'm with Mike. "I've gotta go." Hendrix didn't look well. I suggested a cab. "Yeah, that'll be great. Can you get one?" This was about 2am. I led him downstairs. "Are you OK, Jimi?" Hendrix just says, "Yeah." His voice was slurred, but I saw a lot of people like that. He could still stand, just about, with me holding him, and that was something, in this business. I stuck him in a cab and thought nothing of it.

The way I heard it, a few days later, Jimi moved into a little hotel down in Notting Hill, the Samarkand, on Lansdowne Crescent. Even wrote. A song there, a song he never sang, 'The Story Of Life'. Ironic, that. Tragic, too. On the 18th, an ambulance is called to the Samarkand just before midday. Jimi was a DOA, dead on arrival.

It was exactly like Epstein. I was sitting at home watching TV with Margaret. Just eating my tea. Baked beans, nothing fancy. And the newsreader's telling us Hendrix is dead. Bloody hell. First Brian Epstein and now Jimi Hendrix. I was beginning think it was the Weaver curse. But I stuck with it at Apple. What else could I do?

The Beatles' court case got started at the beginning of 1971. Another

Graffiti-covered door of Apple's offices in Savile Row, September 1976. The caption reads, "The end of a legend"

strange period. I went down to the High Court with Allen every day. Every single day. And do you know what? Klein loved it. I took Klein to a few fights at Wembley, and he was really into movies and theatre. I guess he loved drama. Now here was the biggest drama of the age, the bust-up of The Beatles. The end. I think he liked that attention, and also the excitement of the case, fought out by two legal teams and Klein at the heart of it.

I only remember seeing Paul in court. A funny little courtroom, not like you see in the murder trials. I'm not sure the other Beatles turned up. They sent their affidavits and that was it. Phoned in their evidence. Paul was neatly dressed, in a suit. Klein was also suited up. He was the businessman. Both were fighting for the soul of The Beatles.

Allen hadn't been happy when he discovered that Paul wanted to get Linda's dad in as the band's manager, but a lot of people still thought The Beatles would work it out. Even though they were going to court against each other. There was that big karma thing. The vibe, man. Perhaps I thought that, too. It's too final. So I was shocked when I remember Klein telling me that the court case would finish The Beatles. "This is it," he'd say. "This is the end of The Beatles." And Klein was all for blaming McCartney, big-time. He was certain McCartney was tearing the whole thing apart. But Paul got his way in the end. A receiver was appointed and they went their separate ways.

I've still got a file, which makes sad reading now. All the stuff – "fixed assets", they called it – that John, Paul, Ringo and George bought before the end of December 1970. In other words, what made Beatles and co. There are the four Beatles Mercedes cars in there, the odd Steinway upright and a bunch of other instruments. But it makes sober reading. All Apple Corps had left after the band split. Apart from the music, that is.

Item	Cost
Rosewood desk with black leather inlay	£136. 12. 0
Mercedes Benz 600, BPH 600H	£14,243. 3. 2
Radford stereo amplifier	£94. 0. 0
Stroboscope	£45. 0. 0
Harmonium	£27.15.10

Model 401 recorder/reproducer with NAB Dynatrack Electronics
with 1" tape, four-channel DYNA eight-track NAB with one C0023
1" eight-track erase head, one C0025 1" eight-track
playback head   £8,843. 5.0

16 noise-reduction system	£4,134. 0. 0
Pair of headphones	£47. 6. 0
Rhythm Acc automatic drum unit, serial no 162044	£147. 0. 0
Mercedes Benz 280 SL coupé, AMP 11H	£4,880. 4. 9
Radford amplifier	£94. 0. 0
Thorens TD 135 turntable	£40.18. 0
Moog synthesiser	£5,193. 1. 2
Leslie unit for use with Fender amplifier	£80. 0. 0

Then there was the stuff that remained untraced:

CKF 2/SS Wingate Royal (ex-Peter Brown's office)	£96. 9. 2
Bagpipes	£150. 0. 0
Rosetti guitar	£106.18. 0
Three special French collapsible shoulder braces (made by Moustic)	£112.10. 0
Mercedes 230 SL, GGP 196C	£2,975. 0. 0
Mercedes 230 SL, HEL 296D	£3,446. 1. 4
Fender dual amplifier	£373.16. 0
Fender VI bass guitar, serial no 218111	£243. 1. 6
Fender Jazz bass guitar, serial no 246147	£218. 5. 4
Fender Princeton amplifier	£105.19. 6
Two Ludwig short drums and stands	£160. 3. 6
Fender Precision bass guitar, serial no 229098 (with case)	£119. 4. 5
Fender Mustang bass guitar, no G251B (RS)	£167. 0 .0
Rolls Royce Phantom 2, GH 2845	£1,750. 0. 0
Semi-acoustic guitar, Fender G2776, serial no: 226254	£220. 0. 0
Beomaster 900m amplifier	£65.16. 9
J-160E Gibson guitar with case, serial no 855638	£107.17. 4

Four untraced bass guitars. That was a lot of missing guitars. Who played bass, again? I guess Paul didn't feel like giving them back. I also wonder if those bagpipes were his, something he used to fool about with on his Scottish farm? I couldn't imagine George playing them. Nor John.

BEATLES & CO.

FIXED ASSETS IN POSSESSION OF THE PARTNERS WHICH WERE
PURCHASED BY THE PARTNERSHIP PRIOR TO 31ST DECEMBER, 1970

Items confirmed by Apple Corps Limited 27th October, 1972 as in their
possession

			Cost			
A	1	48" Diameter Rosewood circular table	£	58.17.	0
A	2	M60D Rosewood Refrigerator		164.	0.	7
A	3	Rosewood desk with black leather inlay		136.12.	0
A	4	SW59A Rosewood and leather chair		45.15.	0
L	5	Mercedes Benz 600 BPH 600H		14,243.	3.	2
L	6	3 drawer filing cabinet (bought 1968/69)		38.	9.	o
L	7	Bush T.V. set		330.15.	0
L	8	Ferrograph Model 633/H Tape Recorder		131.	5.	0
L	9	Record Mixer		52.	5.	0
L	10	Radford Stereo amplifier		94.	0.	0
L	11	Thorens TD135 turntable		41.	0.	0
L	12	Ampex 1100 Recorder		149.10.	0
L	13	2 Tannoy York Loudspeakers		162.	0.	0
L	14	Tauberg Microphone		6.	5.	0
L	15	Formica Instrument Board		266.14.	6
L	16	6-Channel Grampian Mixer		94.	4.	0
L	17	6 Recorder Wooden boxes		36.	0.	0
L	18	Beyer Microphone boom		67.	5.	0
L	19	Plastic cover on lounge sound equipment		70.15.	0
L	20	Stroboscope		45.	0.	0
L	21	Sony T.V. MN/990 UB		84.	5.	0
L	22	Harmonium		27.15.10	
L	23	Model 401 Recorder/Reproducer with NAB Dynatrack Electronics with 1" tape, 4 channel DYNA 8 track NAB with 1 C0023 1" 8 track erasehead, 1 Coo24 1" track recordhead and 1 Goo25 1" 8 track play-back head		8,843.	5.	0
L	24	Nagra, without synchroniser		483.	2.	0
L	25	16 Noise Reduction System		4,134.	0.	0
L	26	Pair of headphones		47.	6.	0
L	27	Kodak Carousel slide projector		79.13.	6
L	28	Instamatic ML8Q projector		75.	0.	0
L	29	Bellow Howell Model 8652 projector with speaker unit (serial No_600248)		354.	2.	6

List of some of The Beatles' assets bought prior to Paul filing for the dissolution of the band

CONTRACT OF EMPLOYMENT

BETWEEN Abkco Industries Inc ("The Company")

and

A. Weaver. ("The Employee")

NOW IT IS AGREED as follows:

1. The Employee is employed as Chauffeur by the Company.

2. The employment is determinable by either party by at least two weeks' notice in writing provided the Employee shall have been in continuous employment for more than six months. Should the Employee be continuously employed by the Company for a period in excess of 6 years, the period of notice shall be four weeks.

3. The remuneration of the Employee shall be £ 1765 per annum and shall be payable weekly in arrears, any alteration to be notified to the Employee in writing.

4. The normal working hours of the Employee shall be 10 a.m. to 6 p.m. Mondays to Fridays. One hour daily is allocated for lunch to be taken generally between the hours of 12 noon and 2 p.m.

5. The Employee will be entitled, in addition to the usual public holidays, to three weeks' paid holiday in each calendar year provided that the Employee has been in the Company's continuous employment for twelve months. Should the Employee not have been in the Company's employment for at least twelve months the Employee shall be entitled to one weeks' paid holiday provided that the said employment shall be more than six months. The said holiday must be taken during the currency of a calendar year and will be taken at times convenient to the Company.

6. (a) On bringing into account the amount of any National Insurance benefits receivable, provided that the Employee shall have been in continuous employment with the Company for more than twelve months, he shall be entitled during any period of absence from work due to sickness or injury to a total remuneration of 4 weeks' salary, in any consecutive twelve month period. If the Employee has not been in the continuous employment of the Company for such twelve month period but has been employed for a continuous period of more than six months then he shall be entitled to a total of two weeks' salary.

(b) Any Employee who is absent from work without permission and without good reason acceptable to the Company will not be paid for the period of such absence. The Company may at its discretion pay the first two days of absence through illness without a medical certificate being produced. A certificate shall be produced by the third day.

Above: Alf's contract with Abkco
Below: His redundancy package, 1985

abkco INDUSTRIES, INC.
Registered Office:
2 Chandos Street, London W1M 9DG. Telephone: 01-580 4571. Telex: 27894

ABKCO INDUSTRIES INC.   28 June 1985

Dear Sirs,

This will confirm that you have offered and I have agreed to accept the sum of £4,000.00 in full and final settlement of any claim I may have against you for loss of employment resulting from the closure of your United Kingdom operation.

I hereby acknowledge receipt of the sum of £2,646.00 on account of the said £4,000.00 and agree to accept payment of the balance of £1,354.00 on 31 August 1985.

In addition to the above, you have agreed to purchase for my use the office rental car, registration no: DJD 445V, at a cost of £540.00.

Yours faithfully,

ALFRED CHARLES WEAVER.

Even though I did a lot of freelance work, and had set up my own business by the early '80s, I remained on the Abkco payroll until 1985. That's when Klein finally shut down the UK office. I got four grand and a car, but not that old Beatles car. Shame, that.

7 Good Times, Bad Times

I first met Peter Grant in 1965. Mini skirts and mini cars. Purple hearts and power chords. I liked Grant. He was born in the same year as me, both 30 at the time. Like me, he'd been dragged up on the streets, packed off for evacuation. He'd also done some wrestling back in the day. We had a bit in common, me and Peter. We hit it off. We could talk the fight game.

But we could also walk it. Grant certainly could. Grant was enormous, even then. A big bastard. Two hundred and fifty pounds of tough London beef, and I never saw him scared. Rough and tough as hell, when he needed to be, although that was often. In those days, some fuck was always on the hustle, coming up short, taking the piss, seeing what they could get away with. In Peter's case, that was fuck all. He didn't take shit from anyone, least of all when cash was involved. And he wasn't going to take any shit from some two-bit operator who ran a poxy theatre in some Godforsaken town. I heard he'd had all sorts of run-ins. Supposed to have pistol-whipped some music-hall manager who'd come up short after a show in the '50s. Probably could have collected a bit of time on the back of that. But he didn't.

Grant didn't just act as manager; he was head of the family, a brother to the band, and also their hit man. By the time we met, he'd done them all, worked with Little Richard, Gene Vincent – sweet Gene Vincent – The Animals, mostly as tour manager or road man. Now he was with The Yardbirds. As I said, by the time I walk in to the set-up, Eric Clapton has walked out. As I heard it, he couldn't stick that song 'For Your Love'. Thought it sucked myself. Jeff Beck had been around for a bit. Now he was gone. Guitar was Chris Dreja, Jim McCarty on drums, Keith Relf on voice. And Jimmy Page on psychedelic guitar. It's amazing the sounds he got out of that guitar, because you'd be hard-pressed to get him to say anything. Quiet. Very quiet. But a real gentleman. Jimmy Gent. Not one of those snide bastards.

In those days, The Yardbirds were always at it, out playing. Grant wound them up and stuck them on the road. He made them work for their money, but he always made sure he got it for them, too. Some managers would be too scared to put the muscle on a theatre manager if he was holding out, worried they might not get asked back to play. Not Grant. Fuck that. "What's the point of playing if we don't get paid?" he'd ask. He would have crawled over broken glass to get his wedge. So, if a promoter needed squeezing, he would go in strong. The takings would soon pop out. I know this because I was with him a few times.

The first time this happened, we were down in west London, out near Ealing. Page and the boys had played a gig there a few days back. For some reason, Grant hadn't collected the money the same night. Maybe the guy had disappeared or had given Peter some bull. It was only a few quid. The Yardbirds were big, but the takings weren't always, not after everyone had skimmed off their bit. Taken their cut. But the way Peter saw it, his "boys" had earned it, and he wanted it. He'd heard enough excuses already. Time to cough.

Grant called me and I picked him up. "This bastard's there tonight, Alf. I've already rung to check. We'll get our money...and a bit more." Grant wanted his pound of flesh. I didn't doubt he'd get it, although I wondered why I was going along. Grant could handle anyone. Maybe he thought he should give more time to management and let someone else do the heavy work. Couldn't see it myself, though. He loved steaming in.

On the way down, Grant told me he'd called this promoter and put on a camp voice. "Pretended I was a bleedin' iron with a fairy band that wanted to play his fucking shithole." I couldn't imagine that. "Couldn't wait to meet me, could he?" We laughed at that. Dumbass promoter. He was going to wish he hadn't crossed Peter Grant.

I remember driving around looking for that theatre hall. All the time, Peter was running through what was going to happen to this guy. "There's the place. That's it, Alf. Stick us over there." We parked up outside. It was late afternoon. Grant was out of the car first. Always in first, that was Grant. He was going to enjoy this. We burst into the theatre, up a flight of stairs and *bam!* straight into this fella's office. It was like one of those films where the secretary comes running in after us. "I'm sorry, Mr So-And-So, they just ran straight past me..." This guy was behind his desk. Little fuck. Stupid waistcoat, hair all over the place, droopy moustache and cords. I remember that – big purple corduroys. "Don't worry, Sheila. I can handle things up here. Give us a minute, luv, and…" He didn't look like he could handle a hairdryer at that moment, but he was probably banging the secretary and needed to put on an act.

Now he's asking if we've got an appointment, but his voice is cracking and I can see his hands. They're shaking. He must have been stupid to hold out on Grant in the first place, but this was plain dumb. "I'll just see to these…"

Grant didn't wait for him to finish his sentence. "I want my fucking money and I want it *now*."

Nothing. This guy just sits there.

"Did you fucking hear me?"

The guy's still not moving. He can't. His secretary is screeching and I'm watching all this, ready to move. But Grant doesn't need me. Behind his desk, the guy has gone very white.

"*Where is my fucking money?!*" Peter and I look at each other. "Or do you want some fucking trouble?"

Still he doesn't move.

Peter slams the desk with his fist. It wouldn't have been fair to smack the little weasel. "Get it, you fuck. *Now!*"

Slowly the guy got out of his chair and edged back towards a cupboard on the wall, facing away from us. There was a little cash box in there. That's what he'd gone for. He counted out what was owed. It can't have been more than a ton. Probably dropped a few fives on top. Then he turned to hand it to Grant. Now we could see why he'd stayed seated for so long. Those cord flares. Remember? The purple ones? They were now drenched in piss.

I doubt that promoter had much future in the music business. He would never come close to booking Grant's next band, Led Zeppelin.

Working for Zeppelin in the mid and late '70s was something else. They were the biggest band in the world, at this point. No question. They'd done it all by the time I caught up with them. I was out in Los Angeles with Mike Nesmith when Jimmy Page discovered Plant singing at some obscure black-country gig. Robert was then making his crust in

Hobbstweedle. That name says it all. But because I'd worked with Jimmy and Grant, I followed their early progress. It was mighty stuff. From The New Yardbirds and 'Train Kept A-Rollin'' to Led Zeppelin and 'Dazed And Confused' in a few short months. I caught them early on their first US tour at – where else? – the Whiskey A Go Go. Mike and the other Monkees were really knocked out with 'Communication Breakdown'. It seemed that they became big overnight, although Bob was getting stick. Percy, they called him.

I never worked with Zeppelin in the States. I heard all the stories about the Continental Hyatt House in LA, the Riot House – teenage girls camped outside doors; I've seen that a few times – and nights out on the Strip at the Whiskey or the Rainbow. The usual rock 'n' roll stuff. And I got a taste of what was going on when they shipped back home.

Jimmy hadn't changed since The Yardbirds. He was always the quiet one. The group had got a rep for busting things up, but little James kept his nose clean. Kept himself outside of that stuff. Bottles, clothes, TVs out of windows – it wasn't his thing. Always in control. Jimmy Gent. And a real rock star. Probably one of the last. He liked the ladies, no question, but always polite.

Robert was Robert. He liked to have fun, did Plant. On a real star trip. Loved the limos, the planes. He was born for rock 'n' roll. But he also had another side, too, that quiet family-man thing, with a farm in Wales. Also a big Wolverhampton Wanderers supporter, as I remember. Billy Wright, Stan Cullis, Derek Dougan, Mike Bailey, and all that. Tricksy stuff at the Molineux ground. Wouldn't stop yattering about them, until they met the Gunners. Arsenal played Wolves in the FA cup a few years back. Must have been when Wolves were something. Me and Robert watched the game and I remember ribbing Percy about that, because Arsenal beat them. That pissed Robert off. But he was a good kid.

John Paul Jones. Bright as a button, Jones. Smart. For me, no trouble at all. Wouldn't know he was around, sometimes. A former session musician, so enough said. But he knew what he wanted, know what I mean? He was never going to burn the house down, but he might get someone else to do it. Like Bonzo.

Bonzo. That was John Henry Bonham. Force of nature. One of Plant's old muckers from around Kidderminster. A former hod carrier, and he played drums like it – wham, bam, thank you Bonham. *Bam, bam, bam.*

What a noise. I used to go down to Olympic Studios in Barnes. Led Zep would be recording, and I'd keep watch and keep the press or a few nosy bastards at bay. This was early on. Jimmy and Robert always seemed to lead – lead the Led – but those studio sessions were always held up by one man: Bonham. He'd stop the ball rolling. Held things up all day, fiddling around with his bass drum, breaking his trees, getting some new ones, having a drink, taking a leak. Then we'd be on to the bars and clubs. This was going to be something. We used to have a lot of trouble with John Bonham in clubs.

Now, Bonzo was a big fella. Not as big as Grant, but big enough. Then there was his voice. Fuck. Always shouting. Always full volume. Number eleven shouting. "I wanna go there. I wanna do this. I wanna do that." He'd get very drunk very quickly – three pints for every one Robert drank, five pints for every one John Paul Jones drank. And this rabbit going all the while. Bullshit, really, but aggressive. He wanted to scrap anyone and everyone. Loved a fight.

One typical place we ended up was the Speakeasy, a group haunt. I'm there. The band's there. Bonham's blind drunk. He's in the corner trying to bust some sap's nose. The way I heard it, Bonzo thought the guy said something to him. "Excuse me," perhaps. Maybe, "Can I buy you a pint?" Bonzo goes steaming in, although, like all these fights, there's more pushing than punching. But the sap isn't giving much ground. There's me and another couple of boys, and now we go steaming in. "He's a bit drunk, mate." This is me to the sap. "Leave it out." All the while pushing Bonzo back out of the way. "We'll get you a drink, sort you out a round." The sap was trying to get around me to land one on Bonham. I could see he'd put a few punches together because John's nose was bleeding.

"Hey," I'm saying, "you know who that is? That's John Bonham of Led Zeppelin. He's just had one too many. We can sort it out."

All of a sudden the sap looks over and sees Plant, Page and Jones sitting in the corner. They'd just carried on drinking, ignored the whole damn thing, like it happened every night. I guess it did. "Leed Seep-eel-an?" Turns out the sap's foreign. French, I think.

"Yeah, mate. Led Zeppelin."

He's eased off now. Then he asks, "I buy Leed Seep-eel-an a drink?"

Bonzo hears this. Doesn't matter that the guy's just tried to knock his

Alf on the bonnet of John Lennon's old car in August 1976. The caption reads, "How to pick up a hitchhiker"

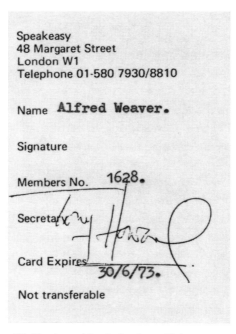

Alf's identity card for the Speakeasy Club

teeth out. "Yeah, I'll have a fucking beer." Bonzo is over again, wiping the blood from his face. But instead of trying to fight the sap, he's got his arms around the geezer. "Wot, Paris? Yeah, we've played there, I think." Plant, Page and Jones didn't look up once.

Bonzo's real partner on those nights out wasn't the band but the road manager, Richard Cole. Ten years younger than me, he'd been with The Who. Scared the shit out of most people, and those that weren't dealt with Grant. That sorted them. A good team, Grant and Cole, in their Chelsea offices. Swan Song, they called them. A little boozer nearby, where the group met for lunch and their pissed-up boardroom meetings. Cole was a nutter. He'd encourage Bonham. "Go on, John. Go on." In the bars, in the clubs. "Go on. Get stuck in. He deserves it." Not that Bonzo needed much encouragement. He'd throw his food, his drink and sometimes punches. He knew we were there. Cole as well. With a few minders behind him, nothing serious was going to happen. He could be Lord Rockstar and no one could stop him. "Calm down, John," I'd say. He wouldn't have any of it. "Yeerrr! Fuck 'em!" he'd say. "Fuck 'em all." That was Bonham's motto.

So I was in and out with Led Zeppelin. They'd go to America and I'd work with someone else. When they were back in the UK, we'd hook up again.

By 1976, punk rock was raging in London and New York. That T-shirt Johnny Rotten wore, where he wrote "I Hate" across the faces of Pink Floyd. Then there was Richard Hell. "Please Kill Me" – he that had on his shirt. Hate and war, not peace and love. 'White Riot', The Clash's Sten guns in Knightsbridge. 'Dazed And Confused', 'Stairway To Heaven', 'Immigrant Song' – I liked them, but they suddenly looked washed up, old hat. The new order was in town, and it was one minute 56 seconds of gob. "Nah, nah, nah, nah, nah, nah." Knives in W11.

But the old dinosaurs were still hiring. Good job. The punks didn't want bodyguards. Bad image. I caught up with Grant and the boys when they rolled into town for *The Song Remains The Same*, Led Zeppelin's film première. Bob, Jimmy, Jones and Bonzo on celluloid. Part occult mumbo-jumbo, part concert footage. That's what I liked. A bit fuzzy, but it was Led Zeppelin at the top, right up there with 'Whole Lotta Love'. Even Grant was in there.

The band's label, Atlantic Records, held a meeting on 8 October 1976 at the company's Berners Street offices. The agenda was *The Song Remains The Same* and the post-première party. Robert Plant was the only band member present, but his contribution was vital. Four different traditional beers would be available at the party, including Robert and Bonzo's favourite, Banks'. Special arrangements were made with the Midlands-based Wolverhampton & Dudley Breweries to deliver the booze. The wine was selected by "that well known connoisseur of the grape, Chevalier du Tastevin Robert Plant". A special bar would also be provided for the exclusive use of Led Zeppelin and authorised personnel. Oh yeah, and "Alfie Weaver will be responsible for the personal security of Led Zeppelin, their families and immediate entourage, etc". Don't know who the etc was.

The group booked into Blakes' in south Kensington. Zep in SW3. It was their hotel, where they stayed when they came in from the country. The way the night played, the film would screen in two cinemas: the ABC on Shaftesbury Avenue and the Warner West End II, just down the road.

We got to the ABC Picture House at 8.26pm. Everyone is seated. Led Zeppelin enter by centre door. Big screams. Up the aisle, up into the circle and into our seats. I give the signal and the lights go down and the film comes on. Led Zeppelin get up, we all troop out, into another limo, down the street and into the next cinema. Arrival: 8.45pm. A few photos. A bit of mingling. Chat chat chat. Keep John out of trouble. We didn't even make it through to 'Moby Dick', Bonzo's big drum blow-out. I gave the signal to the projectionist. He faded the lights and started running the film. Three frames in and we're up and out. Troop over to the party.

The flick bash was laid on in Covent Garden, in the old flower market. This is before it got developed. Atlantic had put me on the Stax tour with Otis Redding, and now the man behind the label was there, Ahmet Ertegun. Lovely fella. I said hello: "I did the Stax thing with Otis. Shame about Otis."

Led Zeppelin parties were non-stop beer (Banks', naturally) and birds (blondes, mostly). There were always a few drugs around, too – a few Quaaludes, speed, cocaine, H – but alcohol was Led Zeppelin's main drug. They were juice men. I don't think I ever saw Bonham without a pint of ale in his hand.

The booze is flowing. There's a cockle-and-whelk stall, a mobile fish-and-chip shop and a bloke on a tea urn serving egg-and-bacon sarnies. A nice little disco, too. And the music is Led Zeppelin. Loud. Good party. Then I see Grant, over in the corner, having a barney with some guy. I thought I recognised the guy, but didn't immediately make him. Ah, fuck it. I knew Grant could handle most things, even the rough stuff.

Then I saw the switchblade come out. The guy has pulled it. Wait a minute. I *thought* I knew him. He was a fucking minder, too. One of ours, but not regular. I'd brought six other guys with me in this job. What's his fucking name? And what's his fucking game? He's supposed to be looking after Grant and the band.

The band? I look over at Plant. Brushing his perm. He's OK. Page, he hasn't seen anything. He's talking black magic with some bird. Bonzo and Jones – who knows where they are? I'm walking now, getting myself next to Peter. "You fucking cunt," this guy's going. Is it Brian? "Don't you fucking tell me what to do!" Grant was having a go. Or at least he was until the knife comes out. I knew the guy, slightly. Jesus, what was his name? Brian? No. Bert? I go, "Listen, mate. Do yourself a favour and fuck off."

He looks at me now. Shit, what's his name? "Why? You want some." The knife is still there. What's he going to do? Stick me?

I was waiting for the lunge, waiting to parry. "Come on, then." Sock him one. Maybe get the knife away.

"You're an asshole, Grant."

I tried not to crowd in. I wanted – I needed – to keep some distance. The fighting distance. Enough to pull a punch. Didn't want to be right on the knife. "Go on. Fuck off and let's forget about this."

I could feel Peter getting ready to make his move. He... It wasn't Bert. Think. *Think.* Ben? Was it Ben? It was a B, I'm sure. He was all ready to have a go. Fuck. I didn't want that. Tomorrow's headlines: "Stabbing At Rock Star Party." Worse, "Led Zep Manager Killed." The guy – not B at all; it's Dave, Dave someone – was looking at us now.

Then I saw it. Fear. Dave knew whatever was going to happen was going to happen soon. Grant the wrestler, me the boxer. Two fighters. He'd got a knife, but that edge was slipping away every second he didn't use it. He'd lost it.

"What the fuck are you going to do with that?" A beat. "Dave?"

Nothing. Dave pockets the blade and mumbles some bullshit. "Yeah, yeah. Fuck off, Dave. It's all over. You're finished."

Grant turns to me. "Thanks, Alf."

I'm watching the guy, seeing that he leaves. "So what was that about, Peter?"

Grant throws me a blank. "You know what, Alf? Fucked if I know." He wasn't joking. "Just like old times, that." It turned out to be a good party. I think I might have sacked Dave.

Three years later, I was standing in a field with Robert Plant. Bob was in a good mood. The sun was shining. 'Ozone Baby'. He'd fished out a favourite red shirt. We were on our second or third fag of the day and we were out of the Smoke. In Hertfordshire. Knebworth, an hour north of London. Led Zeppelin were going to play two outdoor shows right where we were standing. "It's going to be fucking huge, Alf." Robert took off his shades and looked out at the trampled grass.

Yeah, I thought, following his gaze. Just like the Stones in Hyde Park. That was ten years ago now. I was feeling old. "Any Hell's Angels at this one?" Plant didn't answer.

Led Zeppelin hadn't played in England for years, since before the film *The Song Remains The Same*. We were holed up in a hotel nearby and I remember doing a couple of runs to practise the route into the park. In the car going over, the band seemed nervous. This was their big comeback to try and recapture the glory years, scratch back some cred. While they'd been away, punk had been and gone, Johnny Rotten was John Lydon, disco was happening and the Labour Party wouldn't see power again for more than a decade. It was 4 August 1979.

The crowd was enormous. A cliché, this: it really *was* a sea of denim – Levis, Wrangler, Lee. And long, greasy hair. Bonham was taking it easy. Actually, he'd never get drunk when he was working. You'd say to John, "Have a drink when you get to the club," and he did. Or Jimmy and Robert would tell him to knock it on the head until after the concert. They'd crack into the vodka, then. Grant, the wives, Todd Rundgren, Ron Wood – they're all backstage. Chas 'n' Dave, too, they played one of the gigs. 'Sideboard Song'. Rabbit, rabbit, rabbit. Chas spots those 100,000 people and is horrified. "We're used to playing in pubs!" he said. I said, "Go and do your best. They'll love you." What else could I say?

Alf, Robert Plant and his daughter and Jimmy Page's wife at Knebworth, 11 August 1979

Then Led Zeppelin went into a huddle. Funny, that. They always did this big love-in thing before they went out onstage. Hugs all around and then three hours of supercharged blues. 'Celebration Day'. 'Communication Breakdown'. 'Trampled Underfoot'. 'Whole Lotta Love'. People have asked me, "Who's the loudest band?" I can tell you, it's Zep. They were louder than the rest. The Yardbirds were loud, and I've worked with a few hard-rock groups, but Jimmy, Jones and Bonzo came up with the loudest noise through those Marshall stacks. I used to have to put cotton wool in my ears. Ear plugs. And I knew, a couple of years before I finished, that my hearing was getting worse. I've got a hearing aid now. It's a flash one. In my glasses. And I put a lot of that down to being onstage with Led Zeppelin.

The group did the whole Knebworth thing again a week later. I took my son Martin along that time. We went up onstage with John Bonham's son, Jason. He was turning into a good little drummer, just like his old man. Poor John. It didn't surprise me when he died, although it was a shock. A real fucking shock. You get close to someone,

someone younger than you, you think they're going to live forever. But I'd seen a few go by then – Morrison, Hendrix, Brian Jones. It still hurts to see Bonzo on that list.

8 Too Marvellous For Words

Around about the time I was working with Led Zeppelin, I started working with another great. The greatest, some might say. The main man. The main event. Francis Albert Sinatra. Mr Frank Sinatra. First time I saw him, it was July 1950. Remember I said I saw all the shows at the London Palladium? Sinatra the crooner was over in England for the first time. We hit the West End. Caught Max Miller on the same bill, and then Frank. It wasn't quite The Monkees, but it seemed everyone had turned out that night to catch Sinatra do 'Old Man River' and 'A Foggy Day'. Even Ava Gardner was in town.

A quarter of a century later, I was introduced to Frank again. Again, it was at the Palladium, November 1975, and Sinatra was a month away from his 60th birthday. More importantly, he was in London for a week of shows. Thousands had been trying to get tickets for the concert. I thought I'd be one of them. As it happens, I ended up backstage.

Frank was 20 years older than me, but near his best. He had the audience eating out of his hand. "I'm here and it's gonna be booze and broads and all that stuff," he told us. It was like the head of state had come to town, not just the chairman of the board. I'd seen tight security, but this was tighter than tight. Tight as a drum. No one was allowed near Frank, not even his dressing room. We had the whole place stitched up. If someone came around back, they'd better have a good reason. Another thing I remember: Frank had given up the old cancer sticks. It didn't last long, but he didn't want to be tempted back and the order went down that no one was to smoke. That was a tough one. I was still on a pack a day, sometimes more.

I can't claim to have become best buddies with Frank on that job, but he was a real hero and I didn't care. This was something different. I'd never really bothered about working with stars before. Yeah, The Beatles were huge. The Stones, too. But Sinatra was in a different league. I'd got all the records. I'd grown up on them. *Songs For Swingin' Lovers. A Swingin' Affair.* Christ, there weren't many days when I didn't put 'My Kind Of

Town' or 'New York, New York' on the old hi-fi. So working for the man was about as good as it got.

As Frank made more and more comebacks and more and more trips to England, I started to get in with his people, MCT – Music, Concerts and Television – on Beauchamp Place. Harold Davison ran the place, but the company secretary was Liz Pretty and she started calling me. "Alf, Mr Sinatra is in town. Could you handle all the security?" You bet. Ol' Blue Eyes is back in town.

Sinatra always brought over a huge entourage. They'd be his press man, Milton Rubin – Milt. Great bloke. Used to know the Broadway columnist Walter Winchell, the guy Burt Lancaster based his character on in the film *Sweet Smell Of Success*. "Match me, Sydney." Great stories, Milt told. He came up with all the spin. Kept the press happy, or at least away from Frank. That was an important job. Frank couldn't stand newspapers. Hated them and the reporters who worked for them. He thought journalists were always hounding him, churning out drivel. Called them whores. "Those pimps! Those bloodsuckers!" he'd shout. "Get them the fuck away. I don't want to see them or hear them. Vipers!" I don't remember him ever giving an interview or even nodding to a journalist. Milt had a tough job.

Who else came over? Susan Reynolds – she handled publicity. Elliot Weisman, Sinatra's manager and his wife, Maria. Frank's hairdresser, the wig man. He'd always travel with him. Did a good job. You could never tell Frank wore a syrup.

Then there would be Frank's band, the drummer Irv Cottler and his wife, Rose, and Bill Miller on piano and whisky. A drinking man, Bill. Sol Gubin. Of course, Barbara came on the scene around then, too. Her and Frank got married in July 1976. She was a great lady. Never took any bullshit.

In London, Frank and Barbara always stayed at the Savoy. Always. And they always had the same suite of rooms, right opposite Waterloo Bridge. Sinatra's party would occupy half a floor, and we'd have two men at either end of the corridor and two downstairs. Two blokes would stay outside his room, even if Frank and the rest of us were out. I also made sure there was a fresh bottle of Jack Daniel's in his room. Also Chivas Regal, gin, cognac and a few soft-drink mixers. This wasn't any minibar shit; it was a proper drinker's bar. White Russian? No problem. We've got some Polish vodka in there, a little Kahlua, ice and cream.

If guests wanted to walk past Frank's door, we'd tell them it was out of bounds. Didn't matter if they had rooms on that floor. They weren't allowed past Frank's room. "Take the other stairs," we'd say. No one argued. They loved the whole performance. Something to tell the kids. "We were staying next door to Sinatra, and we weren't allowed to walk past his room." Right. With Sinatra, we had to have men everywhere. That could get pretty costly, but Frank's pockets could handle it.

Frank Sinatra – security 1984

Hotel
Four men, 24 hours a day, 14-23 September £1,728

Royal Albert Hall
Ten men @ £20 per show, 17-22 September £1,200
One music man @ £15 per night £90

Misc rehearsals, airports, parties £132
£3,150

The way it worked with Frank, he was always hungry. There was the River restaurant at the Savoy, but we normally went out for dinner. He had a couple of favourite spots: Santini's in Victoria, or a couple of other Italian joints in Mayfair – La Pavona on Blandford Street, Tiberio on Queen Street. Cecconi's in Burlington Gardens was also good. Quiet, intimate restaurants with a bit of traditional cooking. That's what Frank liked. Spaghetti, pasta, rich tomato sauce. A nice bottle of red wine. Frank, Barbara, Davison or Weisman on one table, me on another. Frank always made sure I had something to eat. "Look after my boys," he'd say. "Anything they want, put it on the bill." And we did.

Sometimes, Frank's son, Frank Jnr, would be over, too. He started to take over his old man's band. Then there was Jilly Rizzo. What a guy. Jilly was Frank's right-hand man. He went everywhere with him and became Sinatra's shadow. He started as a minder, like me. Jilly also ran a saloon in New York, where he always kept a free table, the same free table, just in case Frank dropped by one afternoon. No one else sat at that table.

Jilly and Frank were pretty close by the time I hooked up with them. Played poker together, ate together, drank together. They did everything together. Sometimes, Barbara used to get a little uptight about having Jilly around, but he was part of Frank's life. He'd always be at Frank's table.

I remember one time Weisman was over and they were planning dinner for around 8pm, probably at Santini's. I'm outside Frank's room and he's out at seven. A bit early. Probably just woke up and wanted to bum a fag, I thought. Frank's attempt at kicking the weed had come to nothing. Barbara wouldn't let Frank smoke in their rooms. I always thought that was funny, because Frank could get pretty wild about anyone telling him what to do. But he'd come out all meek. "Got a light, Alf?" Sure. We'd often have a little smoke together. He gave me one of his lighters, once. It had his signature on it and we'd stand there in the corridor having a couple of crafty tabs.

"Where is everyone?" I thought he was going to blow. "I think you're a bit early, guv'nor." I always called Sinatra "guv'nor". He liked nicknames, and this was his British one. The guv'nor said, "Well, I'm ready, so let's get going."

That was the thing about Sinatra – you couldn't change his mind. "Come on, guv'nor, let's go into the bar." The Savoy had a nice American bar. I knew we could get a drink or two down there.

"Two Jack Daniel's, barman." Coming up. So me and Frank Sinatra are sitting at the bar, shooting the breeze. Couple of JDs on the rocks. Me and Sinatra! The biggest entertainer in history. I'd worked with all of the music greats by this time, but Sinatra was another level. He was everything – showman, performer, Mr Entertainment. His whole life was in the spotlight, and now I was there at the Savoy bar sharing some of it.

Sinatra was always into small talk. He'd known royalty. He'd known presidents. JFK had been a friend, once. He'd known every Hollywood star worth knowing. But he seemed happy just shooting the breeze, talking sport. "Football – you know, soccer?" Sinatra didn't get the thing about supporting Arsenal. "Sounds like a crap game, Alf." I couldn't convince him. Boxing, that was Frank's game. He loved the fight game. Tyson was coming up big around then. He looked invincible. But Frank's real hero was Jake La Motta, the Raging Bull. "He was Italian, Alf. Like me." Sinatra was raised in Hoboken, across the Hudson River from Manhattan. La Motta was born nearby, in the Bronx slums. "We came up the hard way. It was tough on those streets."

Sinatra told me his old man and a couple of his relatives had been boxers and that he often went to Madison Square Garden. "Friday-night fight night, they called it. It's the best sport, period. Fuck soccer." I couldn't agree with that, but this was Sinatra. I let it go. And he really knew his stuff. He did a

With Frank Sinatra at the Royal Albert Hall

whole number on La Motta. He identified with him completely. I gave him the old tales of Camden Town – "Catholic; can't be too many of us" – and my boxing. He liked having a fighter on his team. We ordered up another round of Jack Daniel's and he told me about his son, Frank Jnr. Frank was part of the Sinatra team, but he was living in his dad's shadow. Anyone would. Frank worried about that, the usual father-son stuff. After that, we were like old buddies. "Hey, Alf. How're your boys, the Arse-sen-all? Is that right? How're they doing?" Great, Frank. Just great.

That's how it was with Sinatra. Chatty, if things went well. He could be as sweet as pie. But if something bothered him, that was it. Like a bomb exploding. He could behave like the worst bar-room bully.

Take the time we went to the Royal Festival Hall in 1981. We've got a fleet of Mercs all piling across the river. Frank is in a Mercedes up front. Black. We jump out and steam into the hall. Frank's appearing there and wants to rehearse. We're heading for the main theatre and this guy tells us we're going the wrong way. "I'm sorry, the theatre is being used by the ballet. You'll have to use the Waterloo room."

I could see Frank was going to blow. He looks around at me, then back at the theatre guy. "Don't fuck with me." The guy leads us off. I didn't know about this and just shrug.

Frank checks out this conference room. "What the fuck is this?"

The guy goes, "It's the Waterloo room."

Frank has a fit – "I don't want to sing in a fucking *cupboard!*" – and storms out. "You think you can fuck around with me? Get me out of this place!" We went back to the Savoy and Frank had the management in his room. They were roasted. I could hear him ranting and raving inside. Then he was out for a smoke. "Jeez, what a fucking day. Got a light, Alf?" I got out my lighter. The one with his signature on it.

Another time, I'm in trouble. Right opposite the Savoy on the Strand is a little Catholic church, up there in Covent Garden. Sinatra and Barbara would walk over every Sunday. He was a good Catholic. At least, he liked to think he was, and that's part of the story. The first time, me and a couple of other boys walked behind him. No one ever bothered him. He said England was the only country in the world where he could do that, go to church in peace. "Anyplace else, it's a riot." Frank and Barbara get into their pew and I stand at the back. Nice service. A bit long, but I'd lapsed, and it was nice to be back in the fold. I now go every Sunday with my new missus, Ella. Got back into the thing.

Anyway, with Frank, I'm thinking, No one's bothering him. Next time, I'll slip out and get a few pints in. So next Sunday comes around and Frank and Barbara walk across to the church again. He's inside and I'm off with the rest of the mob – me, Jilly, a couple of others – down to a boozer I know in Nine Elms. We're having a right old time. Couple of whisky chasers. Bit of wise chat. Taking the piss. "Did you see his suit?" "Frank's?" "Yeah, the blue one. Fucking awful." When we get back, of course, the priest has wrapped things up pronto. The show's over and Frank's out. He's been and gone. I knew what I was in for when I got back to The Savoy.

"You fucking bastard! You should be outside that church, or in it. That's what you're paid for." He was really giving me a good lashing. Then, "And next time you do that, if you're going down the pub, bloody well wait for me and take me with you."

The thing that people always ask me about Frank is his Mafia connections. I never got much change out of Frank when I brought this up. In fact, I was always blanked. And judging by the look on Frank's face, there was no point in pursuing it. Best to stick to sports. Keep it light. "Have another drink, Frank?" Sure. "What about Sugar Ray. Did you rate Robinson?"

However, everyone knew Sinatra's path crossed with the Sicilian boys. The infamous gangster Lucky Luciano was supposed to have been a close friend in the early days. Sinatra visited him in Cuba, then denied they were pals. Then there was the time that mob boss Willie Moretti was alleged to have stuck a pistol in the face of Tommy Dorsey when Frank wanted out of the bandleader's outfit. "I suggest you have another look at that contract you got with my pal Frank." He'd played at Skinny D'Amato's 500 Club, in Atlantic City. The notorious mobster Sam Giancana owned part of the 500 Club. And there were rumours linking Frank to the Chicago racketeers the Fischettis.

Did I ever see him hanging out with hoods in England or Europe? There was one time. This is in the late '70s. We were at the Royal Albert Hall. Frank is in his dressing room and says, "Do me a favour, Alf. There's a guy. I want you to take care of him." I knew what that meant – not what the mob meant when they said it. *Take care of him, will you, Shorty? Look after him, Dutch.* Rub him out, that's what it meant. "His name is the Judge." The Judge. What sort of fucking name is that? I thought. But, you know, he was Frank's friend, so that meant a box with a good view of the stage, champagne, Havana cigars, whatever he wants.

Next thing, I look around and there's this guy. Big fella. Slicked-back hair, when slicked-back hair wasn't fashionable. Sunglasses. And this is late at night, inside. Overcoat draped over his shoulders. Good suit. Expensive. He could have been wearing spats. Maybe he was. It was like central casting for *The Godfather*. The Don. "Here's the Judge." He gives me the old two-handed handshake. "Pleased to meet you." Left hand over right. Says *ciao* to Frank. There's some hugging in there before Frank waves him away and nods at me. I was looking for the bulge in the jacket. Couldn't tell under the coat.

The Judge wasn't what you'd call a big talker, but he never gave us any trouble, either, and we did our best by him. More than our best. I didn't want to get on the wrong side of the Mafia. I knew we'd be heading to Italy with Frank, soon. That was their territory.

Frank was always in and out of the UK. And he did this a lot during the '80s. It was through Frank that I met Sammy Davis Jr and Liza Minnelli. At the beginning of 1988, Sinatra, Dean Martin and Sammy got together for one last time. The old clan. What was left of the Rat Pack, doing it again.

Thursday 9-Sunday 19 June 1983   Dean Martin, Apollo Theatre, Victoria

I had worked with Dino in 1983. He'd done a week at the Apollo. Joel Ross on drums, Moe Scarazzo on bass. Mort Vyner was his manager at the time and Wall Street Crash were support. Dean stayed at the Inn On The Park, ate at the Four Seasons. Martin was incredibly laid back. Always had a drink in his hand. Bourbon. He never rehearsed, just used to show up and go on. He'd be at the theatre 30 minutes before the curtain went up, straight onto the stage, no warm-up, and *bang*. But always an unbelievable show. Then he was off again. He never hung around.

So it would have been nice to see old Dino again, but he'd left the tour by the time it hit England. He'd been hitting the sauce after his son died in a plane crash, and him and Frank had been at each other's throats. Again. Liza teamed up with Frank and Sammy.

Monday 17 April 1989   Sinatra, Minnelli, Sammy Davis at the Royal
                                     Albert Hall, London
Friday 21 April 1989   Sinatra, Minnelli, Davis

Frank and Sammy. Great double act. A lot of history there, but that's another book. All the bad blood between Frank and Sammy had flowed. It

Alf takes care of Dean Martin's flowers

was in the past. Now they were always joshing around. Whenever I saw them, it was smiles and a slap on the back. I guess they knew there wasn't much time left for either of them.

I got one of my boys to look after Sammy while I handled Frank. But Sammy never looked well and I remember saying goodbye to him as he left for the airport after a string of dates at the Royal Albert Hall. "See you next year, Sammy," I called. He looked at me and said, "I don't think so, Alf. So long." He was right. A few months later, in May 1990, he was dead. Throat cancer. He was only 64.

Later that year, Frank was back in England for another series of concerts, this time at the London Arena. I'll tell this little story because it illustrates the power of the Sinatra name at this time. He was doing about four gigs at the London Arena, in east London, which is murder to get to. Sinatra's people asked if we could get a police escort down there. Otherwise we'd be stuck in traffic for hours. I wasn't confident. The Queen, she gets a police escort. The Prime Minister, too. But Frank? I went down to the motorcycle division in Euston. "I'm working for Frank Sinatra

M.C.T.

45 Beauchamp Place,
London, SW3 1NX

Tel: 01-581 5822

Concerts being given by FRANK SINATRA

in Madrid and Milan — Sept. 25th and 27th 1986

		HOTELS:
TUE. SEPT. 23rd 1986	Orchestra flies from London to Madrid on Iberia Flight	The office will be at:
	IB 601 leaving London 11.45 a.m. arriving Madrid 14.15	Hotel Ritz, Plaza de la Lealtad, Madrid 28014
		Tel:34-1-2212857
		The Orchestra will be staying t:
		Apart-Foxa 32, Agustin de Foxa 32, Madrid 28036
		Tel:34-1-7331060
WED. SEPT. 24th 1986	Rehearsal in Bernabeu Stadium, Concha Espina No. 5, MADRID.	Ritz and Apart-Foxa 32 hotels
	Time of Rehearsal: 2.00 p.m. (On stage)	
THUR. SEPT. 25th 1986	CONCERT Bernabeu Stadium, Concha Espina No. 5. MADRID.	Ritz and Apart-Foxa 32 hotels
	Concert at : 9.00 p.m	
FRI. SEPT. 26th 1986	Travel from Madrid to Milan on Iberia Flight	The office will be at
	IB 784 leaving Madrid at 10.05 a.m. arriving Milan at 12.05 a.m.	MILAN, Hotel Principe de Savoia, Piazza della Reppublica 17 20124 MILAN
		Tel:39-2-6230

Proprietors: Music, Concerts and Television Limited
Directors: Harold Davison, Gary Davison, Elizabeth Pretty Secretary: Elizabeth Pretty
Company Registered in England No. 1507212 Registered Office: 12 Thayer Street, London, W1M 5LD.
Any offer contained in this letter does not constitute a contract

Above and right: MCT Sinatra schedule, 1986

M.C.T.

45 Beauchamp Place,
London, SW3 1NX

Tel: 01-581 5822

ITINERARY FOR FRANK SINATRA CONCERTS - CONTINUED

		HOTELS
FRI. SEPT. 26TH CTD		The Orchestra will be staying at:
		MILAN, Ciga Diana Majestic, Via Tiave, Milan.
		Tel: Milan 202122
SAT. SEPT. 27TH 1986	MILAN, Palatrussardi, Via Saint Elia 33, Milan.	MILAN, Principe de Savoia and Ciga Diana Majestic Hotel
	Rehearsal will be at Palatrussardi - Time to be advised.	
	CONCERT at Palatrussardi: Time: 8.45 p.m.	
SUN. SEPT. 28TH 1986	The Orchestra returns to London from Milan on Alitalia Flight	
	AZ 458 Leaving Milan at 9.00 a.m. Arriving London at 11.00 a.m.	

and he's doing a few concerts. Can we have an escort from the Savoy to the London Arena please?"

They gave me the official line. "Escorts are only laid on for royalty or heads of state. Singers don't qualify," they said. Well, not your normal singer, but this was Frank. Frank almost counted as royalty. Then they said, "I guess this is Sinatra. Tell you what, we'll think about it."

Come the night of the first concert, we've got two policemen revving their BMWs outside. "Good evening, Mr Sinatra. Just follow us, please." And we did. We left in the rush hour and it took us just eleven minutes to cross London. The police had fixed it so that all the traffic lights turned green as we approached them.

Sinatra maybe forgot the odd line at this stage in his career, missed a note or two. Maybe he wasn't at his peak, like in the '40s or '50s. But even if he was only half as good, he was still a lot better than a lot of other singers. He was *that* good. And that's why he could demand – and get – a police escort.

And his reputation was the same all over. When we were in Milan, the police loaned us one of their men to help our team. The police would come shopping with Barbara. They'd move cars, shift people. They would have changed the time of day, if it had helped Frank out.

23 September 1986	Start of Frank Sinatra tour
24 September 1986	Madrid
28 September 1986	Milan

Probably the best concert I saw Frank or anyone do was at Glasgow Rangers in July 1990, the Scottish football club, in Ibrox Stadium. We had the home team's dressing rooms and Frank was ferried out to the stage in a golf buggy. He was halfway through the concert when he wandered over to me standing off to the side of the stage. "What is it, Frank? You want a drink or something?" Frank pointed to a row of wheelchairs lined up at the side of the pitch. "No. I wanna go down there." This was unheard of. Sinatra going into the audience? It was the sort of thing Bono did. But he was adamant, so I took him down and he shook hands with every person in a wheelchair, all the while continuing to sing. The crowd went mad. His last number was always 'New York, New York', but this time around Frank goes, "Let's do another one. 'Where Or When'. Let's do that." Suddenly all the musicians are looking at each other, wondering what the hell Frank's pulling on them. Normally everything was rehearsed down to the second. Now they're scrambling around looking for the music to 'Where Or When'. We got back into this golf buggy and I drove Sinatra back to the dressing room. Inside, we could hear the crowd cheering for him. They were still cheering when we left the stadium.

9 Hit The Road

I've worked with a lot of acts and groups. Gene Pitney, Spencer Davis, Lulu, you name it. Either watching over them at the venues they played or travelling with them on the road. Up and down the country. Across the water to Europe, America and the Far East. But one of the funniest jobs that sticks in my mind is from the mid '70s. I was in Cardiff with Bob Marley. Rastaman was playing a UK tour. Jah Weaver and the Trench Town warrior in the depths of Wales.

All the roots rockers were in town that night, Guinness Export hanging in a slack hand and a joint in the other. Bob was no different. He had spliff on the go the whole time. If Bob could have smoked sleeping, he would have. And big fucking things, too. He didn't skimp on dope. "Give us a toke, Bob." I'd take a little weed. "Jesus, my head's spinning." Bob would laugh at that. He had some strong fucking blow, and the aroma from the dressing room that night was breathtaking. Literally.

All of a sudden, the pork are outside. The local drug squad is out in force and they want a bust, badly. Get the big reggae star. Put the Rastafarians under heavy manners. "We have reason to believe illegal drugs are being consumed on these premises, sir."

Consumed? I was still feeling the effects of Bob's carrot. "Urrrgh, I'm certain, er, there's nothing going on here, Sarge."

The coppers are trying to push past. "Wait up, wait up," I'm saying. "Mr Marley is, er... He's having a shit." That was the best I could do. I was playing for time. I was also praying, Bob, finish up that spliff, man. I hoped he'd stashed the stick somewhere, because the old bill were getting past me. Not hard – I was stoned. But I follow them into the dressing room. The windows are open, wide open, and the wind's howling around in there. And Bob? Sitting right in the middle, innocent butter-wouldn't-melt expression. "Hello, police officer," he says, giving

With Boy George at the dog track

the old closed-fist salute. "Would you like a free ticket to watch?" The coppers are raging. More *we have reason to believe* bullshit and they turn the place over, but they can't find nothing. "I think all the drugs must be outside, officer." I was right about that. Bob had tossed them out the window, bundled up in a little red, yellow and green package. We picked them up later, after the gig, when it was cool. I was pretty mellow by then.

A couple of years down the line and reggae is taking a back seat. There's a new fashion in town. This is when boys would dress up in a monk's habit for an evening out, feathers in their caps, worn at a jaunty angle over thick pan-stick make-up. Yeah, that's right, the New Romantics. They were ripe for a slapping. Dressed up like the bleeding Queen Mum. But you've got to admire them. They had balls. In my book, no one deserves a cuff around the ear unless they've crossed you. Someone wearing their mum's best powder-blue silk scarf to accessorise a kilt is not a crime. Fashion crime, maybe, but that's about it. However, there was always more than enough headcases to dish it out if they spotted what they thought were a couple of fannies. That's what was happening with this post-punk thing, the cult with no name. They were getting beaten to fuck. Naturally, they stuck together. They went to Blitz, a night club in London's Covent Garden. Steve Strange on the door and Boy George in the cloakroom. Then imagine '30s Berlin crossed with Barbara Cartland listening to Kraftwerk. Enough to intimidate most kids. But not my next employers.

One of the regulars from those dark Tuesday Blitz nights calls me up. "All right, Alf? Listen, we like your style. Let's have a chat about you working for us." This was Steve Dagger. If Epstein was the fifth Beatle, Dagger was the sixth member of Spandau Ballet. A little pretentious – the management company was called Reformation – but I liked them. Their first single, 'To Cut A Long Story Short' – lots of scarves, acres of tartan, tons of make-up, oceans of hairspray, fights with anyone who thought they were poofs – and they weren't. Second album, new single, 'Chant Number One' – zoot suits, braces, cufflinks, DAs and key chains. Very stylish. Into the pop charts and to the top with 'True'. By the time I met them, they'd done it all: they'd moved out of home, they'd done *Top of the Pops*, they'd done the limos, they'd done the premières, they'd bought the flash cars. One thing they hadn't done was get themselves a head of personal security. Another step up the ego ladder, having a bodyguard. Now here I was, playing minder to all five of them. I was relieved they'd ditched the kilts.

Monday 30 April 1984	Meeting at Spandau offices
Tuesday 22 May 1984	Spandau Ballet tour
Monday 28 May 1984	Spandau Ballet Haydock Park
Friday 1 June 1984	Spandau Ballet Manchester

Gary Kemp, his brother Martin, sax-and-sex man Stevie Norman, drummer John Keeble and the voice of the band, Tony Hadley. And get this – they were all from Islington. Lived up around Highbury. North Londoners, like me. Better yet, that meant Arsenal men. Apart from Stevie Norman, who was Tottenham. There's always one. Spandau Ballet had drawn the battle lines with arch-chart rivals Duran Duran to paper more teenage girls' bedroom walls with their posters. My job was to keep the teenage girls at bay. Go figure.

Gary Kemp was the band's leader, no question. He talked the talk. Him

Spandau Ballet with Stacy Young, Holland, November 1986

Alf with Spandau Ballet boarding a plane in 1987

The band bake "Slippery" Alf a birthday cake

and Steve Dagger. He wrote the songs. This was something the High Court would later be called to rule on. And they did, in Gary's favour. I remember some of the guys did moan about the Kemp royalties, but I told them it happens in all bands. If you want the money, write the songs. It's that simple.

But that's another story. Gary might have been the leader, but they all got on. They were schoolmates. Gary was quiet, but if anything had to be said, he would say it. Gary was close to his younger brother, Martin. Two years' difference, but very close. However, where Gary liked to get his own way, Martin couldn't give a flying fuck. Just went with the flow. He wanted to have a laugh. A few women (Martin had his fair share of girls after him), drink, drugs, the whole rock 'n' roll enchilada. If anyone was suited to being in a band, it was Martin. Apart from his fear of flying. Martin was a bad flyer. He used to sit there squeezing my hand until he cut off the blood supply. It was a killer if the flight ever got delayed or we hit turbulence.

John. Now, John was the Spandau Ballet's ladies' man, the one after all the women. He was the drummer, see? Had the drummer's wild-man rep to live up to. As soon as we got into a club, he'd be off. Radar on – *ping, ping, ping*. That's her. Zoom in. Stevie Norman was the joker in the pack.

One time, we were in Berlin. Did Checkpoint Charlie, the Berlin Wall. Went over the Berlin Wall – or at least through it – into the communist-controlled zone. Remember, this is before the wall comes down, and all the East Germans are dressed in brown nylon. The ones that drove drove Trabants. They had four wheels, but that's where the similarity with most cars ends. Stevie couldn't believe how cheap communist Germany was. Cheap drink – a couple of Deutschmarks for a round of schnapps. Spandau Ballet was a boozing band, no question. As soon as we got off the bus, back in the west, Stevie and Martin announce they want a bit more. "We're going back," they say. More cheap booze. Cheapskates. "OK, but you're on your own," I say. There was a concert the following day and I didn't relax until they showed up, looking like they'd drunk East Berlin dry.

I was probably closest to Tony in the band. Tony had it all – tall, dark and handsome. Good looking. And a good voice, too. At least, I thought so. He could also have had any girl he wanted. But he was married. I remember we did an Australian tour and every girl was after him. We told him to enjoy himself, let his hair down. "Come on, Tony. Go for it! The missus will never know." But you know what? Tony would never stray, and I admired him for that. I always thought Tony could have been another Tom Jones, doing a run out in Vegas, maybe Lake Tahoe and the Albert Hall – the supper-club circuit, tickets for big bucks, throw dinner in. I knew Sinatra's people and told them to watch Tony. They were interested and wanted to meet, but at that point Tony wanted to write his own songs and stick with the rock 'n' roll thing. I'm sure he would have made it, if he'd listened to me.

So here I was, not yet at the half-century but not far from it. I was like another uncle, the father figure, the shoulder to cry on when they were homesick, bored, in trouble, pissed off, pissed. At least there was going to be some action. I liked travelling. Come on, world. Bring it on. Hellooooo...Birmingham? Holiday Inn? ATV Centre? No fun, this. Welcome to life on the road. Try the Holiday Inn at Newcastle-Upon-Tyne for size. Then how about the Holiday Inn at Swiss Cottage? It was a relief when we pulled into town and found we weren't staying in a Holiday Inn.

Fortunately, there was some overseas action coming up. I got hold of the tour schedule. Milan, Madrid, Barcelona. That's more like it. I took Spandau to the Louvre, in Paris. Then the Vatican. (Well, I'm Catholic aren't I?) We saw the Pope. We went to Pisa. We got pissed. We met Prince Charles and the late, great Diana, Princess of Wales. That was a good night. The Prince of Wales had his Prince's Trust charity, which Spandau had worked for. I remember Charlie comes over. A meet and greet. He sees me after shaking hands with the band. "And what do you do?" I gave him the bodyguard bull. "Oh, my." He looked over at his own security. "I have a few minders myself, you know." I knew. You couldn't miss them. All thin-lipped, ex-army types with bulges under their jackets. "Yeah, but they all carry guns and I don't need to."

The band also had an Asian tour on the books at the end of 1984.

Saturday 10 November 1984	Spandau Ballet concert, Tokyo
Sunday 11 November 1984	NHK Tokyo
Thursday 15 November 1984	Sun Plaza
Friday 16 November 1984	Osaka Festival Hall

The band were hot, but I thought I'd drum up an extra bit of support for them in Japan. Every ticket sold, and all that. I belled my brother's daughter, Tracy, a model in Japan at the time. And what do pop stars like more than Jack Daniel's and coke? Good-looking birds. "Here, you heard of Spandau Ballet?" Tracy thought her Uncle Alf had gone mad. Who hadn't heard of Spandau Ballet? "OK, do you think any of your friends would want to come to some of the shows and after-show parties?" Are you fucking *joking?* Tracy didn't have a problem persuading her model friends to turn out.

But they had a lot of competition. Girls were everywhere I looked with Spandau. We'd hit the clubs and girls would crawl – literally – all over the boys. We didn't pay for a drink all night. Tokyo, Osaka, Fukuoka, Nagoya and back again. One night, we hit a club full of Yank marines. Big brutes in their khakis. Buzz haircuts, muscles, tattoos, full of saké and Japanese girls all around them. Then Spandau walk in. They're not at the bottom of the stairs before the girls have dropped those soldiers and shot over. Good move for the boys. Not for me. The marines start glaring over. Uh-oh.

That night there was only me and Big Russell, another minder. "What are you drinkin', ladies?" they say. "Please, scotch whisky, single malt." The band haven't seen the stares from the marines, but they're still coming. I can see one or two of the boys are itching to take a pop band apart. They call over a waitress and I imagine the conversation as they point over at Kemp and co. "*What* ballet? Come on, guys. These limey fags are some sort of dance troupe."

I look back at our table. The band and the Japanese skirt are pouring scotch down their necks. "Another round over here."

The looks were getting uglier by the minute. In the old days, I might have fancied a go, but I was facing down half a dozen highly trained killers with a former butcher as back-up. The odds weren't good. Rule nine, paragraph 3.4 in the Art Of Minding manual is, "Always know when you're beat." We were beat, all right. Paragraph 3.5 is, "Take avoiding action." Fine, but what? I looked at the band, drunk and draped in girls. They weren't in the mood for moving. I looked back at the marines. They glared back. I dashed across the club and searched for a pay phone out back, by the bathrooms. I don't recall how I found the number for the military police, but I did. "Get down here now! It's all going to go off,

With Spandau Ballet

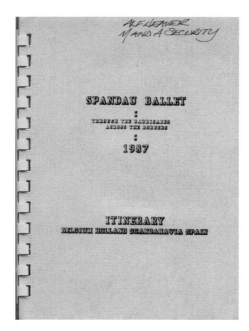

SPANDAU BALLET
THROUGH THE BARRICADES.... ACROSS THE BORDERS 1987

TOUR PERSONNEL

		BAG
THE BAND	GARY KEMP	1
	MARTIN KEMP	2
	TONY HADLEY	3
	STEVE NORMAN	4
	JOHN KEEBLE	5
	TOBY CHAPMAN	6
	GILL O'DONOVAN	7
	SUSIE O'LIST	8
MANAGER	STEVE DAGGER	9
AGENT	IAIN HILL	10
TOUR MANAGER	JOHN MARTIN	11
PRODUCTION MNGR/SOUND ENGR	LARS BROGAARD	21
LIGHTING DESIGNER	PATRICK WOODROFFE	22
STAGE MANAGERS	PETER HILLIER	23
	JURGEN LEIPOLD	60
VENUE SECURITY	ALF SAMUELS	16
BAND SECURITY	ALF WEAVER	12
	NEIL HAMILTON	55
	QUENTIN PIERRE	15
WARDROBE MASTER	ALAN KEYES	14
KEYBOARD TECH	TONY SMITH	24
DRUM TECH	ANDY PEARSON	25
GUITAR TECH	LIONALL WARD	26
STAGE CARPENTERS	VINCE FOSTER	27
	STEVE PORTER	31
RIGGER	PETER RAYEL	30
LIGHTING OPERATOR	SIMON RICKMAN	56
VARI LITE TECHNICIAN	DAVE HILL	33
LIGHTING CREW	BOB BATTY	35
	MARK ENGLAND	36
	TIM PHILLIPS	57
MONITOR ENGINEER	BRIAN COLLEER	37
SOUND CREW	TED LEAMAY	38
	LAWRENCE DUNNETT	40
	CHRIS ADDISON	41
	PAUL JOHNSON	61

Spandau Ballet's 1987 tour itinerary

mate." Within minutes, a bunch of MPs rushed into the club and escorted the marines away.

I picked out some beach beefcake to help me on the Australian tour. Body builders, but they'd do. We did Brisbane, Perth, Adelaide, Melbourne and Sydney. Stevie did a bit of surfing. Loved the sun, sea and surf, did Stevie. In Sydney, our driver gave us a quick guided tour. "This area's King's Cross." Just like London, I thought. "And that over there, that's where the prostitutes hang out." Yep, same as London. "Oh, man, someone was murdered just by that building last night. Maybe you can still see the blood." Terrific. "And we had a stabbing a few blocks down, earlier in the week. Here we are. This is your hotel." Where were those nice Holiday Inns when you wanted one?

We were in Oz for about a month. Now, this is when life on the road becomes tough. All the Koala parks in the world don't compensate for leaving your friends and family thousands of miles behind. Touring is a hard life – different hotels every night, driving for miles. And heavy partying. Spandau made sure of that. (On one tour itinerary, the instruction "Too much to drink, please, barman" was printed on the front cover.) However, I enjoyed the travelling and getting paid for it. But it was hard work. Band security means you're always looking after the band. Never off duty. When you're on the road, you live in the artists' pockets. You put them to bed, you wake them up.

I used to take the room at the end of the hotel corridor and I'd leave my door open so I could watch and hear the comings and goings. Gary often had a piano in his room, or I could hear him trying out guitar chords for a new song. But the pattern for most tours I've been on is pretty much the same. You just fine-tune some of the options to suit the locale. In Oz, this meant the beach, beers, feed the emus, beers, football, feed the koalas, beers, feed the kangaroos, *EastEnders*, beers. The emus would take bread out of our mouths. That was OK for the crew, but I drew the line at Tony trying it. His mouth was his trade, and the headline "Gig Cancelled: Emu Bites Spandau Singer" isn't good PR.

Football was also a good choice. I can't overstate how important football is to a touring band. Yeah, we checked out a few Aussie-rules football games, but it's not the same as a six-a-side-crew-versus-band fixture backstage. I played with the band – left side, as usual. Tony was always centre half, because he was the tallest, and Martin was the striker. Not bad, as it happens.

Here's part of a day's routine that was put out during a European leg of a tour. It just about sums up what we were about, except for the attempt at humour:

Good morning. Actually, if you've got a headache like mine it certainly won't be good and you'd rather it wasn't morning. We leave for Rotterdam at 1.30pm today and drive to the crew hotel to watch *EastEnders* and then the Arsenal v Spurs game live from the UK. It seems that most people support Arsenal, but there's always someone who's got to be different, isn't there, Steve? Scarves, rosettes and Stanleys will be available at reasonable rates from Slippery Alf Weaver.

Yeah, that's me. Spandau nicknamed me Slippery because I always had a habit of slipping into places I shouldn't have been.

Coronation Street and *EastEnders* were favourites. The band loved the soaps, and Keeble's mum would tape a few weeks' shows and send them over in a box, wherever we were in the world. That was always a highlight, seeing Vera and Jack Duckworth get stuck into a pack of tabs and a pint at the Rover's Return. It made us pine for wet Friday nights in the Smoke.

After lunch, there would be more of the same or possibly some promotional stuff – an interview with the local radio station, photo session with a pop mag. There was always loads of press lined up. Gary and Tony were the ones everyone wanted, which left Mart, Stevie and John more time for football. Not that Gary and Tony had a tough time. The questions were always the same. Before each interview, I always said, "Remember where you got the band name, Gary?" The journalist would stroll in and right on cue, "Can you tell me, Gary, where did you get your *fantastic* name?" As it happens, a mate of the band from the Blitz days had come up with it, but that didn't stop the band inventing any number of fictions.

Around four in the afternoon, we'd trudge over to the venue for the soundcheck. The band would then sit around in the dressing room waiting for the curtain-call a few hours later.

Showtime. John Martin, the tour manager, would come in: "Come on, it's about time you lot got ready." The band would tell him where to go, throw things at him. Martin was always onto me, always having a go. Always wanted to be the big man. If he had a bad night, I knew I'd hear from him. I was tempted to quit one tour because he was giving me so much grief, but Gary and the boys persuaded me to stay. They also told John Martin to turn it in.

Tony always gargled for about 15 minutes before he went onstage. He used to use honey, but it sounded like someone was drilling for oil. That drove everyone mad. Then onstage. 'Highly Strung'. 'I'll Fly For You'. 'True'. 'Through The Barricades'. 'Gold'. 'Chant Number One'. All of the hits. Grab a bite to eat, back to the hotel and then the post-gig party.

Parties, the drug dealers' forum. Depending on which act or group I was minding, dealers could be one of a number of things: indispensible, a necessary evil, an unnecessary evil or plain evil. Sometimes, all of those. They're like a cancer. The dealer will crop up at gigs, then at every date, then the after-shows. At one party, out in Australia, I caught a couple of local freelancers trying to push their wares. Nose candy. They had it all lined up on the marble sinks in the bathroom. A mountain of the stuff. At least a couple of grand's worth. I walked in by chance. "What's this?" It wasn't on the Spandau schedule. "Hey, man. Be cool. I've got some good cocaine here." I told them to do it themselves or leave. "What about some for the band?" One of them didn't know when to leave it alone. "Come on, man." I was losing it. "Ah, it won't hurt. Just a little toot. For Spandau, man." I leant down low, as if I was going to do a line. Then I blew the lot on the floor. They went fucking apeshit. A few punches went in, but nothing I couldn't handle.

Gary was always the first to leave the parties, sometimes alone, sometimes not. John and Stevie were the die-hards. But these parties weren't always a major drug and sex fest; some were a drag. But that's part of the business. Schmooze and sell. That day's routine again: "In the audience tonight will be some boring Belgian bastards, journalists, retailers and record company people. At the risk of inducing mind-numbing boredom in everyone, after the show tonight we will be dropping in to a reception held for them. There will be some handshaking and boredom. Tomorrow we travel to Paris, where they are not at all boring, just savagely rude." Spandau kept on smiling through. Fixed smiles.

One thing I never envied Spandau Ballet was when they became tax exiles. The early-morning coach rides might pall. All the hours spent waiting for another plane to another destination may be tortuous. But all that beats sitting in soggy Dublin for a year. Only two months – count them: one, two; that's not many – allowed back in England. OK, the band were going to have a tidy sum that the taxman wasn't due, but Dublin in the rain. God knows why they picked Ireland. Don't get me wrong, I love Dublin, but there's the south of France, Spain, Mexico, California. All inviting destinations for a year off in the sun. Just my luck. I got to spend six months with them. Lucky old me.

I was holed up in a hotel called Jury's. The band got themselves flats nearby, but that was one boring time. I know Martin hated it. It was a strain on the relationship with each other and their families. They were only a few hundred miles across the sea, but they may as well have been in Timbuktu. At times, some of them were close to cracking. Yeah, it was like prison: "I can't stand it! I'm going home, Alf." I'd always manage to talk them out of it. "Don't be stupid. You want to lose all that cash?" Then I'd send them off down the Pink Elephant or another club on O'Connell Street to drown their sorrows with the Irish nectar.

We also got up to Belfast. British troops were still on the streets of Ulster and we'd chat to the soldiers on patrol. This is where Gary got the inspiration for their next hit, 'Through The Barricades'. Gary was affected by the experience and spent a lot of this time writing songs. But for the rest of the band, 1985 was like a sentence. One thing broke the monotony: Band Aid. It came at the right time.

In the winter of 1984, Bob Geldof was watching TV. The news. A report about the starving in Ethiopia. Famine had swept the country and little aid was getting through. Bob the Boomtown Rat. He was stunned, but what could he do? 'Rat Trap'. A pop star whose band had seen better days. Maybe he could do a charity record, but the Rats hadn't troubled the charts for years, and that would be like putting a bandage over a gaping wound. Hang on. Wait a minute. Bob knew the record business and he had a lot of mates in it. Could they be persuaded to put aside their petty jealousies and squabbles and work together? But on what? Band Aid. That's good. The name had a nice ring to it. Band Aid is a brand of sticking plasters, but it also had that double meaning of bands giving aid. Putting something back. Nice touch, that. Nice pun.

Bob got on the blower and made the calls. One of the first was to Midge

Ure, the frontman in Ultravox. The pitch went something like this: the pair write a hit song and get all the biggest pop and rock stars of the day to record it – in one day, in the same studio. The single will then sell millions of copies during Christmas, the most competitive period for record sales, and earn a fortune in aid for famine victims. Midge went for it. Surprisingly, so did everyone else, including the public.

I got a call sometime later. Actually, it was Don Murfet's brother, Barry, on the blower. Barry worked as the liaison guy down at Phonogram, Bob's record company at the time. He did all the parties. "Alf, there's a little something going down in west London. Can you handle it?" I pitched up at the Basing Street Studios, near the Portobello Road, in Notting Hill. It was quiet. It was Sunday 25 November. I was in the dark about what was going on. A few acts were going to record something, I'd been told, but I'd been at duets before. I'd been at the 'All You Need Is Love' sessions. That was big. But this was going to be different, I'd been told. This was going to be a very big day. Right. I still knew nothing.

Then Bob and Midge turn up, around eleven. This thing was down to them, and they were looking anxious. "Give us a shout when they start arriving." I was on the door, looking for the first shows, but there wasn't anyone to keep out, just an old bum who had wandered down from Westbourne Park. He was after a light. Then, hello, who's this? Phil Collins, the Genesis singer and drummer. "All right, mate?" Paul Weller, hopped off the number 23 bus. Sting drove himself. "Nice day for it." Yeah, I thought. This is going to be big. Simon Le Bon and Nick Rhodes. Duran Duran were massive then. The studio could fit the people, but could it fit their egos? With pop stars, there's always a scrap over who gets the best rooms, the biggest rider, the longest stretch. But this time around, they checked their egos with me at the door. Kenney Jones, sticksman for The Who. U2's Bono. Paul Young. The girls from Bananarama. This was the complete A to Z of British pop stars of the day. They were right, it was going to be big. Then Spandau Ballet – I'd met them earlier, at Heathrow, off the plane from Germany – arrived in style in a black limo. "Alfie, mate. We're not first, are we?" They'd probably cruised the block. Then the Quo, or what was left of them. Francis Rossi and Rick Parfitt. In blue denim, as usual. They took up their positions, right at the back. Boy George flounced in late.

It was getting nippy outside and the roll-call of acts seemed to have slowed. I wandered inside. It was all action, camera crews everywhere. And there was also a lot of energy. Nervous energy. The best singers and musicians were assembled in one studio, in front of their peers, and they didn't want to fall flat on their faces. There was a lot at stake. But Midge and Bob were orchestrating. No one had seen the lyrics to their song yet. Sheets of them were handed out. I grabbed one. Title, 'Do They Know It's Christmas?' To the point, that. And then, the first line, "It's Christmas time. There's no need to be afraid." Yeah, good hook. Bono was singing that. And then they all come in for the chorus: "Do they know it's Christmas time at all?" That was powerful stuff. I could feel the hairs on the back of my neck. Tony Hadley was up first, a daunting task, but Tony did it, boxed it off nicely, and that set the tone. It took the day to get the whole thing down, and then it was all over the news and newspapers. But they were right, it was a very big day. And single. FEED 1 went straight to the top of the charts.

The promoter Harvey Goldsmith was on the line the following summer. Band Aid had been huge. Now something else was brewing and this could be even bigger. That's why Goldsmith was in on it. He's promoted everyone who's anyone in rock. Pink Floyd, Led Zeppelin, David Bowie – he's done them all. I'd known Harvey for years. He had an office next door to Allen Klein's London Abkco operation in Wigmore Street. If Harvey was trying to impress a business contact, he'd call up to see if I could loan him Klein's motor, Lennon's old Rolls, for an hour or so. Sometimes I'd smarten up and act like I was Harvey's chauffeur. It looked good in his game if he arrived at a restaurant meeting in a white Roller.

Bob Geldof had got Harvey to help put together Live Aid. This was going to be Band Aid but at Wembley, in front of the whole wide world. No one needed to tell me *this* was going to be big. On 13 July, I got up to Wembley early. Before nine, anyway. No cast yet, only the crew, but even at that time there was a buzz about the place. Fax machines. Dozens of phones. Caravans backstage for the bands to use as dressing rooms. And the artists' catering area set up by the Hard Rock Cafe people. Inside they had a massive canvas with the Live Aid logo on it, and every time an artist came in for a bit of scoff I got them to sign it. Goldsmith was also there.

"Hello, Harve." David Bailey, the photographer. He was taking

With Bob Geldof

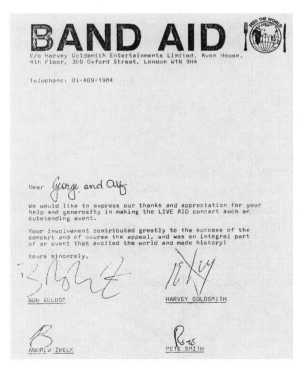

Band Aid thank-you note from
Bob Geldof

pictures of everyone who was taking part in the day. Elvis Costello. Sting. Geldof, of course. The groups were driven and choppered into the stadium throughout the morning. The fans poured out of the tube. I watched from backstage as the place filled. Something like 70,000 were soon packed in and backstage was buzzing. Three generations of British pop music were watching, waiting for their moment. Bowie. Queen. Paul McCartney. "Hello, Paul. Haven't seen you in ages." George Michael. Status Quo. Geldof had queued them up first, the opening act, and they hadn't played together for nearly a year. What a responsibility. And Rick and Francis – normally the mouthiest couple before their own gigs – knew it. They were jittery as hell. Quiet, but pumping adrenaline. I couldn't get two words out of them.

Now I was looking at my watch, counting down the minutes, the seconds. I could hear someone's voice over a monitor. "Ten, nine, eight, seven, get ready, five, four, three, two, one – go, go, go." The PA burst into life: "Ladies and gentlemen, it's Saturday, it's 13 July and it's Live Aid!" It was just turned midday when I pushed Quo onstage. The place blew apart and Francis and the boys ripped into 'Rockin' All Over The World'. That hit the spot. Emotion and adrenaline was pouring out of the crowd. Then 'Caroline'. They closed the set with 'Don't Waste My Time' and the house was up for the next 15 hours.

I watched the whole day unfold from the side of the stage. Style Council. Spandau Ballet. David Bowie. The Rats, Bob's band. And Bob singing 'They Don't Like Mondays'. It was the greatest hits global jukebox. Act after act went on and rocked the house. And then, at nine, they came back for the finale, 'Feed The World', with Bob Geldof taking the bows. "Good one, Bob. Well done, mate." He looked happier than I'd ever seen him, but drained. He didn't look like he could power a ten-watt lightbulb at the post-show party at the West End club Legends, but he gave it a good go and deserves all the praise he got. Well done, Sir Bob.

I've still got the letter of thanks from Bob and Harvey. "Dear Alf," it says. "We would like to express our thanks and appreciation for your help and generosity in making the Live Aid concert such an outstanding event. Your involvement contributed greatly to the success of the concert, and of course the appeal, and was an integral part of an event that excited the world and made history!" Nice to be a bit of history.

10 *Sex And Drugs And Rock 'n' Roll*

Almost exactly a year after Live Aid, I made front-page news. Banner headlines. All over them. Now, that's the last place a rock 'n' roll bodyguard should be. It was all down to a wedding. But it was a big wedding. Bob Geldof's wedding. The wedding of the year. The ex-Rat had just got himself a knighthood. Now he was going to make good on Paula Yates. They were getting hitched. Actually, they'd already done the wedding bit, at a quickie ceremony in Vegas, Nevada. Now they were having second helpings, the blessing. About time, I thought. They'd been together a good while, since Paula was a teenager and Bob was singing about not liking Mondays. They were a great couple. I can't believe Paula's dead now. I still remember her standing in the sunshine, in the garden of their Kent house. It was a priory. Davington Priory. We had some fun that day. The invite read, "The remarriage of Paula Yates and Bob Geldof – Las Vegas/Davington." We did Bob's stag night first.

Friday 22 August 1985	Bob Geldof stag night, Groucho Club
Sunday 24 August 1985	Geldof wedding, 20 men

They closed the Soho media haunt down for a night of boozing, and I remember we tossed out one pop star who tried to crash the bash. I won't embarrass him. "No invite. Out. Now." That's sort of pathetic, isn't it? Bob wanted M&A, our security firm, because he knew we could handle the wedding. We must have taken about 20 or 30 guys down. Be prepared.

A Sunday, and we got there early. A beautiful day in Faversham. We had a couple of meetings with the police. Always did, before a big job, and this was going to be big. "You're going to have to watch out. There's going to be chaos," I warned. I was right. That's what you get when you mix pop stars, a posse of smudgers – all the top boys – a couple of thousand screaming fans, a hundred or so coppers and us in England's countryside.

There wasn't much peace in Faversham that day. Those fans screamed the place down when George Michael arrived in a Merc. Threw themselves at the car. Then they went mad. It was like a Who's Who of stars. David Bowie, in top hat and tails. Very dapper. Bob had said, "I've got to wear a suit, and if I'm going to look stupid, you will, too." I didn't mind, I always wore a suit. Lulu, in her shades. There was the designer Jasper Conran, Terry's boy. He made Paula's dress, a lovely red gown. Same as her daughter's, Fifi Trixibelle. Billy Connolly, the comedian. Sting chartered a chopper. Simon Le Bon. He gave Paula away and read out a message from Prince Charles and Diana. That was nice. Simon's wife, the model Yasmin, and Simon's bandmate John Taylor. Oh, and Linda and Paul McCartney. "Hello, again. How's it going?" Bob's Band Aid mate Midge Ure was there, too. Typical jock, he turns up in a kilt.

So things are set up nicely. Great guests, lovely 15th-century house, parish church bang next door. Quaint little place. St Mary Magdalene and St Lawrence. Bob's got his KBE pinned to his suit. Hadn't shaved, though.

They get married, and then all the aggro starts. We get one plod asking if Bob wants to come out and meet the neighbours. Naturally, Bob says no. "It's a private do. We don't want to be bothered." But that's not good enough. Because Sir Bob's done Live Aid, everyone thinks he's their friend, that they own him. It's always the way. A couple of years before, he couldn't get arrested. Now they want to wish him well. They're moaning about the noise, moaning about the music. To help keep the peace, Bob even turned it down. I wouldn't have. It's a wedding. They're supposed to be fun. Later, I read some idiots were moaning about the "extravagance". Extravagance! They were eating roast beef and Yorkshire pudding. Some didn't like the firework display. A bit too...what? Flash? OK, they spent a few bob on that wedding. Seventy-odd grand, I heard. That's right. But it's their money. No, they're saying, he should be giving that to Ethiopia. Jesus, he'd given more than enough.

So there's all these killjoys moaning. Can't see Paula. Can't do this. Can't do that. You'd think they'd been invited. There's a game of rounders for the guests. I think Bob and Paula won that. And then everyone tucks into the grub. The bubbly is out. It's a right old knees-up.

Everything is just dandy until some joker jumps over the wall. This must have been about 11pm. This guy comes running past, trying to make his way to the house. I don't know who he is, just that he shouldn't be there.

That's my job. I'm a bodyguard. I don't know if he's dangerous or just got a bit excited by it all. "OK, you got me," he says. "Take me out of the front gate." I know all the press are out there, just waiting for something like this to happen, so I said, "Where have you come from?" He points. "Over there." So we dropped him back over the wall, where he got in.

Next day, the tabloids have a field day. "Bob's Bouncers Steal The Show." "Bob's Bouncers Beat Me Up." That was *The Daily Mirror*. "Geldof And Those Guards." *The Sun* had, "Geldof's Minders Beat Me!" We got stick all over the shop, stuff about how we'd manhandled guests, shoved onlookers around, hijacked the wedding. One paper had some of our guys – they called us a "menacing army" – pushing the press around when they were talking to the vicar. "You are getting a bit too busy," they said we said in front of the Reverend Michael Anderson. Then the Rev steams in, said we were "a necessary evil". *The Daily Express* claimed we ruined the big day. "The Bob And Paula Show Is Marred By The Minders" was their headline. "An astonishing war of nerves between police and a heavy mob yesterday marred Bob Geldof's big day." In another paper, there are pictures of me, one under the caption, "The Heavy Mob." Me, heavy? I've never once moved the scales over 160. Newspaper cartoonists got in on the act, taking the piss: "'Still no sign of the bride yet, Sir Bob, only some weird-looking blonde in a red dress. We slung her out.'" Very funny.

The wall-jumper ends up in hospital with a few cuts and bruises. Obviously, that's not good. No one wants anyone to be hurt, but I can't take risks with celebrities. That's what I'm paid for. The guy admitted he was a gatecrasher, but also claims some of the boys beat him up. Bob wants to talk to me, the law want to see me and one copper wants to report us to the Chief Constable. Calls us gorillas. But it blew over. Bob defended us, said we were doing our job, doing what he hired us for, keeping the press and public out. Well said, Sir Bob.

Then, one Sunday, I'm taking the dogs out around Wandsworth and a reporter from *The People* doorsteps me. "Why don't you tell your side of the story?" he goes. Why not? We took a lot of grief on that job and Fleet Street had exaggerated it all, as usual. So I gave him an interview. "We're Not Thugs, Says Geldof Minder." That's me. Not the snappiest headline on the street of shame, but with a nice picture, and they had me down as an ex-boxing champ. I denied the whole thing, all the nonsense that had been written about us being thugs, quick with fist and boot. "My men are hard.

They have to be," I explained. "They're mild, decent guys." OK, I was laying it on a bit thick. "Geldof wanted a private do and we were there to ensure he got one. We were on the inside and the police were on the outside. There was no trouble between them and us. The only trouble was getting a cup of tea and a bite to eat." Keep it light, see. The local rag then got in on the act, but they did a good piece. At the end of the day, it was all about giving one guy a day's peace. Not much to ask. Although too much for some.

It was around this time I started getting into trouble with the wife. The old trouble and strife wanted to go and live in Portugal. She'd met someone else. Margaret had gone on holiday over there with my sister, Ann, and she'd only gone and met some geezer in the Algarve. A piano-player in a club. The marriage was over. I sold the house. We were living at Burntwood Grange at the time, down Wandsworth way. We split the money and I bought a new drum close by on Ellerton Road. Six months later, Margaret wanted more scratch. I gave her another ten grand to keep us out of court. She's still in Portugal. I wasn't too happy with Ann, but I threw myself into the work. Women didn't really figure for me, then. I was always too tired. I was concentrating on work, building up the company.

Good job, too. Madonna landed on our laps the following year. By the time the early '80s rolled around, M&A was the first stop for any celebrity. And I mean *any* celeb. Pop, rock, film, it didn't matter. The phone was ringing off the hook. Stars coming in from the States, France, Spain, Italy, all over. We were working with the world's biggest stars. And they don't come much bigger than Madonna. Nearly 20 years, she's been in the business. The hits: 'Holiday', 'Like A Virgin', 'Lucky Star', 'Papa Don't Preach', 'Like A Prayer', 'Borderline', 'Material Girl', 'Into The Groove', 'La Isla Bonita', 'Express Yourself', 'Cherish', 'Vogue', 'Justify My Love'. Priceless pop. The films: *Desperately Seeking Susan*; *Who's That Girl?*, with Griffin Dunne; as Breathless Mahoney in *Dick Tracy*, with Warren Beatty; *Body Of Evidence*, with Willem Dafoe and Joe Mantegna; and *Evita*. A decade on and she's Mrs Ritchie, wife of the British film director Guy Ritchie.

When I knew Madonna she was with Hollywood bad boy Sean Penn. Poison Penn, they called him, or Mr Prima Madonna. No one had a good word for Sean. He didn't care. He's a great actor, and that's all that counts in Sean's world, doing the work. The call comes in. This is February 1986. Ciccone and Penn are out in Germany, at the Berlin Film Festival, which

THE PEOPLE,

WE'RE NOT THUGS, SAYS GELDOF MINDER

ANOTHER PEOPLE EXCLUSIVE

The People, 31 August 1986, featuring Alf's role at the Geldof wedding

BRAINS BEHIND THE BRAWN: Security boss Alf Weaver

THE man behind the private army of minders involved in the flare-up at Bob Geldof's "wedding" has defended their heavy-handed tactics.

We're mild mannered

Ex-boxing champ Alf Weaver said his tough bunch of henchmen—who are being investigated by police—mind their manners.

"They're mild, decent guys. My men are hard, they have to be—but they're not thugs.

"I'm not saying they're angels either. But they don't go round thumping people for the sake of it.

His musclemen have been condemned by police for their behaviour during the blessing of Geldof's marriage to Paula Yates.

Kicked

And Weaver and his heavies have been quizzed by detectives probing a pop fan's allegation of being beaten up at "Saint" Geldof's party.

Richard McCann, 33, says he was kicked and thrown over a wall after gatecrashing the "do" at

WEDDING: Weaver escorts guest Bowie (left).

By MYDRIM JONES

the Live Aid hero's Kent home.

Weaver, who lives in Wandsworth, London, said: "The Law have spoken to me and some of my chaps, but I don't think anything will come of it.

Private

"This bloke came over a wall and a couple of my men just lifted him back over it.

"It was, after all, a pri-

vate party. He shouldn't have been there in the first place.

"But he wasn't thumped—just helped on his way."

Weaver, 50, who runs M and A Security Services said: "There's been a lot of nonsense written about Geldof's party.

"He wanted a private do and we were there to ensure he got one. We were on the inside, and the police were on the outside.

"There was no trouble between them and us. The only trouble was getting a cup of tea and a bite to eat."

had screened Penn's *At Close Range*. They're coming to London to finish shooting scenes on their new film. It's *Shanghai Surprise*.

Friday 21 February 1986	Madonna from airport BA 378 2305
Saturday 22 February	Madonna's house
Sunday 23 February	Madonna's house
Wednesday 26 February	Madonna at Park Lane Hotel filming
Thursday 27 February	Madonna filming
Saturday 1 March	Madonna and Sean Penn, *Shanghai Surprise*
Sunday 2 March	Madonna and Sean Penn, *Shanghai Surprise*
Monday 3 March	Madonna and Sean Penn, *Shanghai Surprise*
Tuesday 4 March	Madonna and Sean Penn, *Shanghai Surprise*
Wednesday 5 March	Madonna and Sean Penn, *Shanghai Surprise*
Thursday 6 March	Madonna and Sean Penn press conference, Kensington

I knew George Harrison's company, HandMade Films, was producing. It'd be nice to see old George again. Madonna and me, we hadn't met. Not yet.

One night, I found myself at Heathrow. The airport, again. It was like a second home, although it has changed a bit since I first picked up The Four Tops in that old Beatles car. Madonna was coming in on her own. Sean would catch a later flight. I'm there with another M&A guy, Jerry Judge. There's an hour to go before midnight and there's no photographers. Not one. "We're going to be all right," I told Jerry. Ten minutes later, still no lensmen. "It'll be a doddle."

11.30pm and the place is swarming with paparazzi. Richard Young was there, and one of main tabloid smudgers, Dave Hogan. Now, we all knew about Dave. He'd got himself out to Hong Kong to trail Madonna and Sean on location for *Shanghai*. He'd been at their hotel. Tracked them to restaurants. He would have gone to the toilet with them if he'd been allowed, but the security over there blanked him. He was desperate for a shot.

I told Jerry to go in and bring Madonna out a side door leading to the cars we'd got parked up. I could watch them come out, Madonna with her dark shades and a scarf wrapped over her bleached hair. There she is. Jerry in front. The press pack spots her, too, and all hell breaks out, like Madonnamania, the battle between the press gang and the Penn gang. I

Alf with Madonna in 1986

rush to the door, the photographers in pursuit, and I'm trying to hold them off until she gets into the car, me against something like 15, 20 blokes, all firing away with their cameras. *Click, click, click*. Others are shouting for Madonna. "Come on, look up. Look up, girl." *Click*. "Give us a picture. What's it like to be in England? Madonna...Madonna..." No one's going to get any interviews tonight. The flashes were blinding, like in Hitchcock's *Rear Window*, Jimmy Stewart in his wheelchair. *Click*.

I was pushing them back, trying to hold them up while Jerry got Madonna out the building. I knew them all and these guys knew the score. They push, but not too hard. They certainly don't push me out the way, or they know what's coming: a right hook. They know we've got a job to do, basically to stop them and anyone else getting too near. It's sort of an unwritten rule, a code of conduct between minders and photographers. A bit of a game. The celebrity game. Stars can measure their celebrity by the number of photographers that turn out to greet them. Madonna was definitely at the top end.

There was also something else at play. There was – is – another unspoken rule. A tacit agreement. Conspiracy, if you like. The more reclusive the celebrity, the more the press love it. Celebrities who played hardball were always pursued, given more attention. They made the news. They got the column inches. Celebs willing to show at the opening of an envelope...well, they could wait. Just open another envelope. Madonna and Sean in '86 were playing hard hardball. They wouldn't give their mothers a photo at this point.

Back at the airport: "Come on, Madonna. Look up." She didn't. Head down, walked straight ahead, Jerry in front, and into the car. We – me and the photographers – all rushed out, but she was already in the waiting Mercedes. Then Dave Hogan jumped onto the bonnet. Uh-oh. Hogan was desperate for his pics and started to take shots through the Merc's windscreen. Someone pushes him off and Hogan goes flying, gets his foot caught in the limo's wheel arch. It speeds off. Ouch! He's all over next day's papers: "Madonna Madness," "And Speedy Madonna Sweeps Them Off Their Feet!" *The Sun* led with the story "Maimed By Madonna" with a big picture of Dave on the road, screaming in agony. "Pop queen's Merc mows down *Sun* snapper Dave."

It was getting nasty now. Madonna and Sean wouldn't play ball, and anything between us – Madonna's bodyguards – and the press was getting blown into an all out war. The tabloids were obsessed. They were writing anything, as long as it was negative. And on the other side, Madonna and Sean were digging in. At least Dave didn't sue. I think he thought about it, and was getting all the lawyers calling him with ready-made lawsuits, but we had a pint with him afterwards, sorted it. Good bloke, Hogan. He got his ankle fixed up and Madonna was really upset about it, but things then went from bad to worse. Love/hate relationship? This was hate/hate, and it continued for two weeks. Madonna, Sean, me and Jerry Judge holed up in the pair's rented Kensington house. The press camped outside. Every time we went out, we were followed. One time, I spotted a guy on a motorbike. "Stop the car, Jerry. I think I know that guy." Sure enough, he was from one of the newspapers. We pulled up and I got out. I said, "What are you following us for, mate?" No answer. He was playing dumb. I grabbed the keys out the ignition and chucked them away. Not too far, just enough to give us a chance to get away.

Sean would occasionally go for walks, a stroll around London, which was now a battlefield between him and the tabloids, with me in the middle. He'd go out in a balaclava, like one of those ski masks hit-men wear. It wasn't much of a disguise. Everyone knew it was him, but it kept Sean happy. Or not. As soon as he saw a snapper, he'd unleash a mouthful of gob. I think he loved spitting on them. Jerry would go out front and say, "How many pictures can you possibly want?" Some clown would always say, "Just one more, Jerry." But they never seemed to have enough. There wasn't much room for me to do a job with Sean. He was always threatening the press or attacking a reporter. He could do his own work.

Harrison then decided to call a press conference to cool things down a little, give the press something to write about. At this point, the tabloids were running stories about the rips in Madonna's jeans, Sean's prowess with bricks. The column inches about all the wranglers and us, the security, were longer than those covering Madonna and the film. George had had his fair share of bother with the press – we'd been through that with The Beatles – but it had never been hostile, like with Madonna. "Let's cool it down," he said. I looked at Sean. Nothing would cool him down. Not in those days.

One of the funniest things with Madonna is when we tried to evade the press pack – again. She wanted to go for dinner. I'd got an old Citroën at the time and brought it around in front of the house. There was a high wall and a gate at either end of the drive. Instead of climbing in the waiting limo, Madonna slipped into the back seat of the Citroën. Now, this was the car I used to cart around my dogs, Billy and Zep. Lovely dogs, but not the cleanest animals. There's a ratty big dog blanket on the back seat I used to wrap them in. "Get under that," I said. Madonna took a look at all the dog hairs but duly dived under the blanket. "OK, keep down. We'll get out of here soon." The limo drove off first and turned right out the gate. I started up the Citroën and edged out the drive after it. I could see all the reporters and photographers dashing for their motors and some were already in pursuit. We turned left. About five minutes, later I'm gunning down Park Lane with one of the world's biggest stars in the back seat. Then I hear, "Excuse me? Can I come up now?" It was Madonna. I'd almost forgotten she was there. "This blanket stinks. Can I get up, Alf?" I turned around and saw her peering out from under Billy and Zep's blanket, trying to hold her nose. When I see Madonna now, that's the Madge I see, under the dog blanket, holding her nose.

The thing after the press conference was that everyone got more than enough pictures. You couldn't give a Madonna pic away after that. The interest just died. The press – at least some of them – went somewhere else.

Madonna and Sean could have avoided a lot of hassle if they'd done a few pictures from day one. But that, I've learned, ain't always the point. Hassle creates interest, and that puts bums on seats.

I've survived 30-odd years in the business, which has got to be some sort of record, but one band has stuck – and is still sticking – it out for as long as me: Status Quo. The Quo. Blue denim, three chords. Sometimes four. And hard-rockin' twelve-bar blues. They've out-lived every fashion and musical style that has come and gone since they first picked up their guitars, in 1962. But they've also had a few firsts of their own. Over 50 UK hits, more than any other group. In 1982, the first group to be invited to perform for Prince Charles' Prince's Trust charity. Over 100 appearances on *Top Of The Pops*, more than any other act. The first band to play live in four UK cities in less than a day. And, as I said, the first band to kick off Live Aid. Not a bad little record.

I first met the band in 1981, just one year short of the 20th anniversary. By then, they'd gone from that first hit, 'Pictures Of Matchstick Men' in 1968, to 'Rock 'n' Roll'. And then there was a whole bunch of good tunes in between, including their one and only top-slot single, 'Down Down' in 1975. 'Check What You're Proposin''. 'Whatever You Want'. 'Rockin' All Over The World'. 'Roll Over, Lay Down'. 'Caroline'. 'Paper Plane'. 'Down The Dustpipe'. Those were the songs being played at the gigs I was working at.

Wednesday 26 May 1981	Status Quo, Wembley Arena
Thursday 27 May 1981	Status Quo, Wembley

I was just looking after the concerts, keeping the kids off the stage. In those days, the band had been playing to raise cash to feed their drug habits. Francis had over-indulged in the '70s. Cocaine was his thing. He told me he could take a cotton bud, insert it in one nostril and pull it out the other. Some party trick. Rick Parfitt wasn't a slouch, either, when it came to over-indulging. He was the original wild old man of rock 'n' roll.

But Rick was in a slump around then. Depressed. The world had fallen in on him and his wife, Marietta, the year before. Their daughter, Heidi, had drowned in a swimming-pool accident. He's quite a loner now. Maybe it was down to a car crash he had a few years later. He was lucky, looking at the state of the car afterwards. I'm surprised he crawled out alive. After that, Rick cleaned up big-time. He changed a lot. Now he has his mind on what he's doing. That means no drugs and not a lot to drink.

Rick and Francis had been through everything together. They'd first met at Butlin's holiday camp in 1965. Francis was with The Spectres, the prototype for the Quo, with Alan Lancaster on bass and John Coghlan on drums. Rick was calling himself Ricky Harrison at the time and touring with a couple of twin sisters, Jean and Gloria. They were The Highlights. A couple of years later, Ricky had reverted to his real name and joined Francis. They also changed the band name. Status Quo were born.

Nearly 30 years later, I was with the group as head of security. They'd been through a few personnel changes by then. They'd even split up and packed in the touring once, stopped gigging, before Geldof got them back together for Live Aid. Coghlan had quit in the early '80s and Lancaster had tried to stop Rick and Francis from continuing as Status Quo. That went to court, with Alan claiming that the band shouldn't be allowed to continue without him. Now he was in Oz. So it was Rick, Francis, drummer Jeff Rich, keyboardist Andy Bown and bassist John "Rhino" Edwards. They'd also got themselves a new manager, David Walker. Walker joined the boys in 1989 and was the guy they claim straightened them out. I think they felt it was their last chance, the last throw of the dice, if they were going to continue.

I was also heading for a quieter life by the time the '90s rolled around, and that's what made it special with Quo. Of all the bands around, I didn't feel like the great-grandaddy, the old man at the back. There are always a new bunch of fresh-faced 19 and 20 year olds on the scene, and it was getting more difficult to keep up with their fast-paced lives. The Met Bar one night, Brown's the next, then to New York for a photo shoot. Those days of busting a gut were behind me. I'd leave that to Jerry or some of the younger lads at M&A. But Rick is only 13 years younger than me, and Francis 14. And Jeff and Rhino are no youngsters. I felt more like the older brother to the Quo, not the daddy. We could all be a gang. If not the last gang in town, then the oldest.

This is where I blow apart the myth of sex and drugs and rock 'n' roll. Don't get me wrong, Quo had had all of that in the '70s, but in the '90s they were moving into their mid to late 40s and things had slowed. There were marriages to respect, kids on the scene. (Francis often brought his son

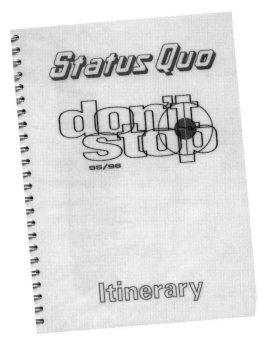

STATUS QUO
Francis Rossi
Rick Parfitt
Andrew Bown 1
John 'Rhino' Edwards 2
Jeff Rich 3
4
5
David Walker - Manager
Simon Rossi - Band PA 6
Alf Weaver - Security 7
Sue Bennett - Wardrobe 8
9

CREW PARTY
Peter Hillier - Production Manager
Dave Salt - Stage Manager 11
Andy Taylor - FOH Engineer 12
Pat Marks - Lighting Designer 14
Tim Franklin - Monitor Engineer 15
Tonto - Guitar Tech 16
Andrew Carman - Drum Tech 17
Marcus Viner - Backline 18
Liz Adshead - Production Assistant 19
Bryan Wilson - Rigger 20
Bill Irving - Sound Systems Tech 21
Arturo Ollandini - Vari-Lite Tech 22
Craig Hancock - Lighting Tech 23
Paul Tibbles - Sound Systems Tech 24
Finbar Neenan - Sound Systems Tech 25
Sam Dineen - Lighting Tech 26
Sarah Muir - Caterer 27
Jo Dennis - Caterer 28
Haden Donnovan - Promoter Rep UK 29
Dave Sowden - Band Bus Driver
Ted Hewitt - Crew Bus Driver
John Curtis - Crew Bus Driver
John Gordon - Truck Driver
Ian Silver - Truck Driver
Andrew Mellor - Truck Driver
Bob Plested - Truck Driver

WEMBLEY   Show Day   Saturday 16th December '95

Band Party travel to Wembley (120 miles)

Crew Party check-in to Hotel after show*

Band & Crew Hotel: **Hilton National**
Empire Way
Wembley
Mddx
HA9 8DS

tel: 0181 902 8839
fax: 0181 900 2201

contact: Lorna
facilities:

to venue: 5 Mins

load-in: 8.00am
sound check: 4.30pm
dinner: 6.00pm
doors: 6.30pm
DEAR JOHN: 7.30pm to 8.15pm
changeover: 8.15pm to 8.45pm
STATUS QUO: 8.45pm to 10.30pm
curfew: 11.00pm

promoter: MCP Promotions Ltd
16 Birmingham Road
Walsall
West Midlands, WS1 2NA
tel: 01922 20123
fax: 01922 725654
contact: Maurice Jones
prod. mng: Haden Donnovan tel:
local prom: tel:

venue: **Wembley Arena**
Empire Way
Wembley
Mddx
HA9 0DW

tel: 0181 902 8833
fax: 0181 900 1055

prod. tel: 0181 902 0883
0181 902 8833 ext (prod.)

fax: 0181 903 2699
manager: Andrew Young
prod. mng: Jeff Goodband
capacity: 10,800

☞ * Crew hotel only for those who require accommodation

Status Quo 1995/1996 tour itinerary

Simon along as the band's personal assistant.) And in 1997, disaster struck again for Rick. He was rushed to hospital and had to undergo a quadruple heart bypass operation. Francis was also losing his hair. The band needed to slow down.

So by the time 1996 rolled around, we were all ready to launch into Europe, but at our own pace.

Monday 27 November 1985	Don't Stop tour, Status Quo, Apollo Theatre, Manchester
28 January 1996	Status Quo and The Beach Boys, Brixton Academy, London

Denmark, Finland, Norway, Germany, France, Holland. Sure, when we were in Amsterdam, Rick and I bought some dope in a coffee shop and rolled a couple of joints, but mostly the lads were tucked up in bed by 10.30pm with a mug of cocoa. I was going to bed later than the band. Unheard of. It was like the Old Cronies tour.

One incident summed up the boys perfectly. We were out in Holland and a group of screaming girls were outside, mobbing the hotel. "OK, no sweat, lads," I said. "I'll get you through this." Rick and Francis looked at me like I'd got a screw loose. "Um, Alf, I wouldn't…" These musicians. I'd show them how a pro worked. I walked out to push through the teens. But before I got near them, they suddenly melted away. They'd spotted the object of their affections running off down the street, and it wasn't Rick Parfitt or Francis. I turned to see them laughing at me. Their days of being mobbed by schoolgirls were long gone.

There were also the big Jane Fonda workouts before every gig. Where most bands would warm up with a few beers and a bottle of whisky, Status Quo were in their dressing room doing exercises. I knew they'd wanted to clean up, but I'd never seen this before. Francis and Rick started doing push-ups in the dressing room. And then Jeff and Rhino started getting into it, getting themselves a small set of free weights. Squats, thrusts, bicep curls, shoulder presses, lateral pulldowns. Jeff would run around puffing and panting: "Come on, lads. Hup, hup. Put some effort into it. One, two, three, hup. One, two, three." After I stopped laughing, I pitched in with a few suggestions of my own, some of the stuff I'd learned from my boxing days. I was surprised they had the energy to go onstage.

Alf with Status Quo's Rick Parfitt at the Hard Rock Cafe in 1991 celebrating Alf's 25 years in the business

Then there was all the sightseeing. 'Whatever You Want'. But with the Quo, that didn't mean lap-dancing clubs or night clubs. No late nights. Sightseeing with Quo actually meant sightseeing – stately homes, historic buildings, museums. On days off, we'd race up to Whipsnade Zoo or some other wildlife park to check out the animals. Francis was a proper Dr Doolittle. Loved his animals.

On the tour bus, we'd do the football stuff. That was good, because Rick, Jeff and David Walker were all Tottenham Hotspur fans. That's like putting a fox in a cage with a hen and expecting them to get on. We had some good old bust-ups when the big London derby with Arsenal came about. Rhino was Brentford, so that didn't count. Then they would get the cards out. OK, now we're talking. A few hands of poker for some big-money stakes. No fear. Didn't even play for matches. All the magazines were about cars or guitars, never Swedish porn, and the videos were comedies or thrillers, never skin flicks. And then, to top it all, I'd spot Andy Bown engrossed in a chess game – chess! – with Rhino. What's the matter with these boys?

However, one of the strangest episodes came in early 1996. BBC Radio 1 banned Status Quo records. The nation's favourite decided that playing anything by Status Quo was unhip. It went against the station's playlist policy. Radio 1 had got rid of the old dinosaur DJs like Simon Bates and Dave Lee Travis. Now it wanted to get rid of the dinosaur bands. Why they picked on Status Quo I'll never understand. What about The Rolling Stones? Rod Stewart? All older than the Quo. It was OK to play Oasis, whose music is anything but original – Beatles rip-offs, really – but, crucially, younger. They weren't losing their hair. Or at least, Liam and Noel Gallagher weren't.

I thought the decision was ridiculous, but Radio 1 was doing anything to try and recapture the country's youth and update its image. Naturally, Rick and Francis were pretty pissed off. They're placid sort of guys, most of the time, but this decision really bugged them. "Let's get this sorted, Alf." They picked me up from my Hammersmith office and we headed off for Radio 1. Round one of the dinosaurs versus Radio 1 had already taken place, with the band and David Walker hosting a press conference. Walker was threatening a judicial review of the radio station. There was talk about going to court. "If the public put Status Quo records in the charts then Radio 1 has a duty to play them," David argued.

God knows why they wanted me around. It was unlikely that any of the station's DJs were going to cause the pair trouble. I'd seen a few of them, and it looked like they had trouble handling more than one CD at a time.

We staged a sort of mini protest, me, Rick and Francis, lined up outside with our placards. "Play Status Quo. Play Status Quo." A couple of photographers turned up to take shots, and a delegation of Radio 1 people in combats came out. This was it, the battle of Portland Place. But far from fists flying, everyone stood around shuffling their feet while hearing the Quo's complaints. That was about it. It was all very civilised. And very silly, really. However, the Quo got more coverage in the national press than they'd probably had before, and the man on the street thought the BBC was being stupid. Radio 1 still don't play Quo records. Who cares? A lot of other people do.

11 *Behind The Velvets*

Rock 'n' roll bodyguards didn't exist when I started out. Security was for presidents, not pop stars. Not rock stars. Minding just wasn't important in the early '60s. More innocent times, perhaps. A few bobbies about. They'd handle it. No one would want to hurt their idol, would they? Sure, there were screamers and there were fainters, and undoubtedly there were a few weirdos about, but not killers. John Lennon's murder changed all that.

And then the bands got bigger, the venues got bigger, audiences got bigger and the number of sickos, jerks and plain evil bastards in those audiences got bigger. Security became an issue. It became a job. In the early days, it started off with driving the stars, offering them a shoulder here, an arm there, if there's any argy-bargy. I might have earned myself a free rum and coke that night in Brixton at the Ram Jam Club, keeping an eye on Otis Redding, but it got so you couldn't do both, driving and minding. I had to choose. I chose minding. The first rock 'n' roll bodyguard. And now, three decades on, the music minding business is booming. It's a multi-million-pound industry. In today's market, a top rock bodyguard can and does expect to pick up a few hundred for a few hours' work, maybe more.

Don't get me wrong, security will never take priority over getting laid, getting drunk and getting high, but getting a good minder is higher on a pop star's agenda than it was 30 years ago. Somewhere between landing an invite to Madonna's next birthday party and buying the latest-model Ferrari. Good rock 'n' roll bodyguards can also be hard to find. It's like a good hairdresser or nanny.

That's why I eventually got around to starting my own company. I'd been freelancing, working for myself for years. Then, sometime in the late '70s, I met a bloke called Mike Conway. Mike used to work at the House of Commons. Not a politician; he was in the post office down there. Solid citizen, Mike. I reckoned Mike and I could be a good partnership. He was a good front man; I was good with my fists. We'd make a good team. We became M&A, Mike & Alf. I wanted Alf & Mike, but that would have been A&M. Someone had already got that. So, M&A Security Services Limited. "Security for parties, concerts, etc." That's what it said on the card.

We started off at Mike's sock on Darcy Road in in SW16. In fact, we were all over the shop for a few years: at my place in Wimbledon, in Florence Road; at Burntwood Grange, where the papers caught me after the Geldof wedding; in Marylebone Lane; then St Stephen's Mews, in Bayswater; and finally, a little mews office in Hammersmith. The work was pouring in and I couldn't believe how quickly the whole thing took off.

Within a few years, we'd made it into the toffs' magazine *Tatler*. July 1984. A feature on fame and the famous. I wasn't on the list of the most famous people in the world, but M&A were among the best-known fame-servers, down there with TV chef Anthony Worrall-Thompson, the crimper John Frieda, Johnny Gold from the famous London night club Tramp and the king of the paparazzi, Richard Young. "Genial Alfie Weaver" – don't know who wrote that – "and Mitchum lookalike Mike Conway, rocking evenly on their springy minders' toes," it said.

By the mid '90s, Mike had left. His wife died and he packed it in for a quiet life on the south coast. It didn't matter. By that time, I'd already recruited a guy, Jerry Judge. I knew Jerry could take over my mantle. I knew he was going to be a good man, and I was getting a bit past it then. My brother had brought Jerry along to a Frank Sinatra concert in the early '80s and I took him on. Of all the men who passed through – and there was a lot – I could see Jerry was the man to take the company further. He was ambitious, well liked. So I taught him the trade, and he got good. He's now the best in the business. Probably the best bodyguard in the world, now. Every Hollywood movie star or director asks for him when they come to the UK – Spielberg, Sean Connery, Arnie, Stallone, Bruce Willis. I eventually made him a partner. Even changed the company name. Still M&A, but now Music & Arts Security Limited, not Mike & Alf.

So things got good. In 1997, *The Mail On Sunday* newspaper had got me listed amongst the top 50 groovers and shakers in the music industry. There's Alan McGee, the Scottish bloke who discovered Oasis. My old mate Harvey Goldsmith is in there, too, and Vince Power, the Irish guy behind Mean Fiddler. And then me. "It's a central fact of music-business life: either you're on the guest list or you're not. And if you're not, Alf Weaver will keep you out." They said I was one of "the biggest fish in the goldfish bowl". Favourite single: John

Alf, Jerry Judge and one unknown do their business at Kensington Place

With Mike Conway (far left), partner in Alf's first security company, Mike & Alf

L-r: chef Anthony Worrall-Thompson, hairdresser John Frieda, photographer Richard Young, Tramp owner Johnny Gold and Alf, voted top celebrity helpers in *Tatler*

Lennon's 'Imagine'. Still is. They'd got me on a salary of £75,000, but they didn't know I was paying myself bonuses. I ain't saying what they were.

So what is it that makes a good minder? "You just have to be built like a brick shithouse," people sneer. Wrong. "Just hang around looking hard." Nope. If that was the case, how come I'm shorter than some of the stars I look after? And I've been in the game something like 30 years. I know it inside out. I was minding before there *was* minding. It's a profession, now. There should be a trade union. There isn't. Not even a rule book. So I'm writing it. Makes sense. I made them.

A good minder is born. Sure, like most things, you can train people up, put them on courses. And I've done that. I've trained a few bodyguards myself. But this isn't like cooking or fixing cars. There is a physical aspect to the job. You've got to be able to scare the pants off people and beat seven bells out of them. That means you've got to be able to handle trouble. Not everyone can do that.

Now, I'm not big. Believe me, people are surprised that I'm not six-four and 17 stone. But that's the last mistake they've ever made. I can handle myself. However, the general rule of thumb is *massive bloke = frightened people*. That's what I mean about minders being born. Nowadays, if a minder doesn't duck when he walks through a doorway, he ain't going to be taken seriously. I was lucky. I helped start it all. But if I hadn't been around 30 years ago, I doubt I'd have been given an interview nowadays. Too small.

So, size. It's important, but not the last word. If a guy comes to me and he's not six foot plus, that's not the end of the story. He could have trained as a fighter or got a bit of chopsocky under his belt. That'll go in his favour. Someone who knows how to hit – *whack*, one punch and they're down – are going to be more use than a lardass. Doesn't matter how big he is. Also, a trained fighter is going to have a better sense of how to control situations and the level of force necessary to contain it.

Contrary to most people's impression, a good bodyguard will also be a grey shadow, discreet and unobtrusive. Someone who won't be a target in their own right but can react if anything happens. Now, that's going to be kind of hard if you're seven feet tall and 350 pounds. And temperament – that's innate, too.

So that's what I mean about being born. It's no good having a minder who's a fucking lunatic, lashing out and hitting people all the time, knocking them out for no good reason. The lawsuits will come flying in. But then again, you don't want a big nonce, some soft lad who wouldn't say boo to a goose.

Drinking is also a big no-no. You need men with discipline, and it helps that they're not carrying a load all night, pissed up. Drunk. Fighting is the last thing you want to happen, but it's bound to go off once in a while, and the rozzers are likely to be called if things go real bad. What's going to happen then is the police will nick anyone who looks incapable. So don't drink or order a Shirley Temple. If you're sober, you point and say, "He started it, constable," and you'll get away with it. I have for years. This is what happened a lot with Led Zeppelin and all the situations with John Bonham. Sometimes I'd hit a trouble-maker and the management would call the police. I was always in a stronger position, because I wasn't completely Scotch mist.

Observation and alertness are also highly valued by me. My old minces are going a bit now – I've been wearing the specs for a few years – but it hasn't stopped me watching. A good bodyguard is going to need to be able to keep his eyes and ears open at all times, every single minute they're on duty. It's the old adage: the second you look away is the second that something happens. Now, this sounds easy, but try keeping alert for a few hours at a time. The bodyguard may be on for ten-, twelve-hour shifts, sometimes longer, and he's going to have to keep watch all that time. Then, if he sees something, he's got to assess the risk, the possible implication of taking action or not.

It's also no good just keeping an eye on the artist. It's what happens to them you need to worry about, and that means having to look all around. Onstage, that means looking out at the audience. It's difficult, trying not to catch a glimpse of Bono belting one out or Dino crooning, but whenever I saw one of my men looking at an act on stage, I'd warn them, "Do that again and you're out." And if someone tried to get onstage, I didn't care who it was. If they were trying to get onstage and hadn't been invited, I'd get rid of them.

Nothing, absolutely nothing, can be taken at face value. You always have to be on the look-out for weirdos. And they can come in any guise. I don't even trust young, twelve-year-old girls. They might think it's cool to sleep with a rock star, but that could turn into a compromising position. That's a bad position, if the press get to hear about it. "The Schoolgirl And The Drummer." Those sorts of headlines could make Fatty Arbuckle's fall from grace seem tame. I always expect the worst. I am surprised less that way.

One of the fans' favourite tricks is to find out what hotel a band is staying at and book a room. That way, they're close to the band. I remember, on a Spandau tour in Italy, we had a couple of girls getting jobs as chamber maids. They took hours dusting Gary Kemp's room. There

Escorting Kylie Minogue

With Shirley Maclaine, November 1990

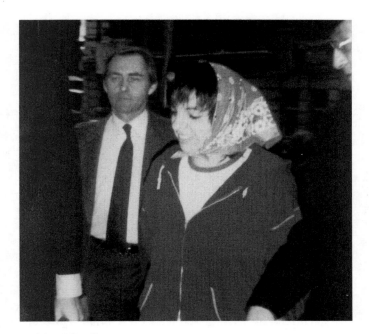

With Liza Minnelli

With Cliff Richard in HMV

wasn't much we could do about them, not until the band left the hotel for a gig. Then the girls would be stuck back at the hotel cleaning the other guests' rooms.

There is also the old fake fainting routine to get backstage. A lot of fans would fall flat and we'd rush to pick them up, take them back and give them some oxygen. They'd be up in seconds, looking around, and I'd know it was just a big con. But better to be safe than sorry.

A good bodyguard will also be able to plan and prepare. The better prepared, the easier it is to take preventative measures. On a big film première or high-profile opening, where a lot of celebrities are expected, I'd always work everything out on paper. How many men. That depends on the celebrity count, the size of the crowds, the venue. Could be up to 30, for a big bash. Then where to place them. Cover all entrances and exits. At least a couple on each. Then do the fire escapes, on the roof, and also the toilets – could be someone hiding there. Also, always a few experienced minders to manage the VIP area. Don't want any trouble there. Sometimes I might assign certain celebs their own personal security. Naomi Campbell gets Brian. Donatella Versace has Mike. Paul gets Kate Moss. Always add a couple of floaters on top of that. They're for emergencies – checking the crowd, settling the paparazzi, that sort of thing. Then I would run through a list of the boys I was going to use, give them the brief and times to be there – always a couple of hours before things kicked off.

I'll be liaising with the police. Maybe they'll lay on an escort. There may also be some special security guys attached to a film star's company. They'll need to be in the loop. I'll talk to the limo company. Who's doing it? And how many cars? Then I'll check the equipment. How many radios? Probably works out one between two men, 15 radios for 30 guys. Get them the security tags, backstage passes, laminates. Pens, pencils, markers, notebooks. Also, if there's a special dress code, I'll tell the crew what to wear and where to get it.

Often I would also draw a rough sketch of the area showing the venue and all the roads around it. Local knowledge is important here, so it's often useful to visit the venue at least once before the big night. Check back entrances. I'd always make sure I knew where the rear exit in a restaurant or club was. I always look out for it. I've taken numerous bands out through the hotel kitchens. I'll even find the back exits in shops, just in case. The Dorchester Hotel has an underground car park, which is great for an easy escape. I think I used that with Diana Ross, a couple of times. However, calling a place to find out where the exit routes are can backfire. The papers are always putting people on retainers to tip them off, and someone working at a club or bar may get wind of what's going on and call the press in. By the time you and the celeb turn up, half of Fleet Street is parked outside.

You need to be methodical, because I've known a lot of jobs go pear-shaped. Maybe crowds have blocked roads and the only available exit route is a one-way street. That needs to be planned for.

I'll know the route the celebrities are taking from their hotels, the direction the limousines are coming in from, where they park up and the path the celebrity takes from the limo to the venue. It may only be a few yards, but anything can happen. I'll know where the crowd-control barriers are going to be erected, which roads will be closed by the police and where the press are going to be stationed. In short, I'll know everything. Whatever. Something will still go wrong.

Arnold Schwarzenegger Première, Warner Cinema, Finchley, London

16.00hrs. Arnie leaves Dorchester Hotel to Battersea Heliport. Chopper seats seven people. Takes off 19.00hrs to Alexandra Palace. Then by limo with escort to cinema

Arnie due at cinema at 19.30-19.45hrs. He will get out of limo, walk through crowd, past press pens, onto stage for photos. Into cinema, auditorium four. Drink and interviews, then out of exit door, down two flights of stairs to limos parked at back of cinema

You can't be too star-struck, either. Treat stars with kid gloves until something happens. Then do whatever it takes. And I mean whatever. Robbie Williams isn't going to mind you ruffling his hair if it means you've stopped someone from slugging him in the face with a can of Special Brew. I've been rough with the best of them, bundled a few into cars. Madonna, for instance. I even had to get tough with Roger Moore, once. The eyebrow wouldn't shift from his seat. "Come on, Mr Moore. Time to go." Didn't budge. He wanted to catch Sinatra singing 'My Way'. I had to half drag him out.

Even the big guys need some protection. When Frank Bruno was the heavyweight champion, I asked him what he needed me for. It was obvious, really. It doesn't make good publicity to have a champion boxer swatting away his admirers, but we can do that for him. And we can tell autograph hunters to clear off. Any star that does that won't last long. I also heard from a friend in the business that Muhammad Ali got frightened when he was rushed by fans.

The paparazzi are a big part of the minder's brief nowadays. I've had my fair share of run-ins. But it's always important to find out if the film star or singer wants their pictures taken. Some, like Kylie Minogue, don't mind one bit. Some, like Frank Sinatra, mind a lot. If the artist is shy, it's best just to have a quiet word with the photographers. "I don't want any pictures, boys." None of them are going to take any notice of that, but the line has been drawn in the sand. They know that, if they take a picture, I'm going to try and stop them. I'll put myself or my hand in front of the camera, push the photographer away, anything. The worst photographers are always the freelancers. They're the ones causing the problems.

Often, security can also find itself playing piggy in the middle of the fame game. The management of up-and-coming groups will tip off newspapers about where a band are staying, eating or clubbing. However, the record company might have employed me to keep an eye on the band, keep their noses clean. We'd tip up somewhere and, surprise surprise, it would be full of photographers. But that's the name of the game.

It's always a question of trying to out-fox them. Difficult, because they'll work in packs, watching and waiting, phoning each other if they have a sighting. They'll also try and follow, in a car or, more commonly, on the backs of motorbikes.

I was once stuck in a traffic jam with a band. We were being followed. I noticed a couple of cabs either side of the limo and had an idea. I jumped out and slipped the cabbies a fiver each if they held up the traffic for a few minutes while we inched forward. We eventually made it.

We've also tried splitting bands up or putting celebrities into even disguises. Sometimes it works, sometimes it doesn't. I once had Spandau dressed in long coats, dark glasses and caps. They ended up looking like bad Marlene Dietrich impersonators and drawing even more attention to themselves.

It almost goes without saying, but the best bodyguards are going to be the ones you can trust, the ones you can leave your mum with. Spandau Ballet used to tip all their jewellery into my pockets before they ran onstage. The band always knew they'd get their stuff back. It was like putting their gear in the bank.

Good minders are also going to need to keep it buttoned. I've had to hide secrets, keep affairs from wives. That's not a nice task, but you've always got to remember who's paying the bills at the end of the day. I wouldn't betray those secrets, even now. A lot of security firms have confidentiality agreements, but in my experience they're not worth the paper they're written on. Either you can trust a guy or you can't. You've got to make a judgment on whether the guy you've taken on will sell someone down the river for a few grand. Hard call, but it's got to be made. Obviously, I've made a few mistakes, had to get rid of a few bad apples in my time. But I've always acted quickly. They've been out, gone. Maybe I've put the guy on a rear exit and five minutes later he's not there. Goodbye.

Sometimes it can work both ways. If an artist or someone in the band gives me or any of my team a present, we declare it. A bit like politicians. I can't tell you the number of times someone has been given a pair of cufflinks or a watch by a drunken drummer who wants it back the next day. "Hey, that guy has stolen my fucking watch!" It's going to get ugly, unless you've got a piece of paper from the management saying it was a gift. If the drummer keeps up, give him the watch back.

A minder also needs patience. The work can often be tedious and routine. I'm all right standing at the front of a venue, watching the limos roll up, or on the arm of Michelle Pfeiffer, but what about the poor bloke standing at the rear exit all night in the rain? He also needs to be thick-skinned, because the results of our job are often seen to be negative. We're there to keep people out of the stars' faces, and that's not always nice.

Eventually, security will or should become second nature to a good bodyguard. A lot of it is common sense, and a cool and logical head is going to get you out of most situations. The experienced minder will be flexible and use the resources they have available to them. They'll learn to guard against loose speech and keep all documents and records under lock and key, or at least out of sight of prying eyes. I always worked on the need-to-know principle. If a guy was working a side entrance at such and such a venue from 17.00 to 00.30hrs, that's all he needed to know.

It's a demanding job, so the best bodyguards are going to have a mix of these qualities and skills. Assuming he does, he's going to be pretty good. But that's just the start. The real job is to prevent an attack, not to deter one once it has been launched. However, there's always going to be some incidents that can never be planned for, and this is when the bodyguard's training comes to the fore.

Once someone has lunged out of the crowd, the minder will need to react instantly and fearlessly to snuff out the trouble. Usually, the best way is to get in the way or shield the celebrity. This will create an additional target and divert the attack. Alternatively, hit back. Hard. Neutralise the attacker, as they say in the States. The celebrity then needs to be quickly removed from the scene. That sounds straightforward, but it means the bodyguard is going to have to assess the threat, decide his course of action and then react with the appropriate level of physical force, all in a split second. Now tell me you just have to be built like a brick shithouse.

That's the minding game pretty much nailed. But later on in my career, I also did a lot of work behind the red velvets, the ropes, working at parties and premières.

18 May 1994	Bruce Willis party
13 March 1995	Clements Ribeiro fashion show, Brazilian embassy
30 April 1995	Prince opens shop in Camden Town
29 May 1996	Ministry Of Sound party
6 August 1996	George Clooney at Planet Hollywood
4 October 1996	Abbey Road Studios, anniversary party
21 August 1997	*Q* Awards
1 October 1997	*Nil By Mouth* film première
18 May 1998	BAFTA party
5 August 1998	*Armageddon* première, Odeon, Leicester Square

On the door. Bouncing. If you're name's not on the door, you ain't coming in. Now there are a hundred different names for the same job. Doormen. Doorhosts. Coolers. Protection specialists. It don't mean shit. They're all one and the same. We're there to bounce people out if they haven't got an invite or they turn ugly.

But it isn't all plain sailing on the other side of the velvets. Try standing out in the cold for eight hours straight picking the cool kids from a crowd of losers. And then there are some basic rules to being a top bouncer. Number one: be nice, until it's time not to be.

First off, the doorman is the most visible aspect of a security set-up, so he plays a crucial role. He sets the tone for the club or the party. He's going to be the first person any guest or clubber sees. It's not a great

Alf's Mission Impossible laminate

advertisement to have a couple of meatheads out there on the pavement at a high-class charity function. That's why I always dress up – black dinner jacket, black cummerbund, white shirt, black bow tie, nice clean shoes. It's better than jeans and a T. A well-dressed doorman is always going to make the customer feel like the place he wants to get into is worth getting into, not some two-bit south London drinking den.

Contrary to popular opinion, the doorman isn't simply there to eject people, chuck them out. He's there to let people in. But only the right ones. A good club or party will always need people to make it swing, but a responsibility comes with that. People want a safe, trouble-free place. The doorman is there to ensure that happens, to stop the pushing and pulling, check that those people who are invited get in, that those who aren't don't.

Also, a good bouncer needs to be able to spot and stop anyone who looks likely to cause offence or is completely boozed up. People have often said to me, "Yeah, I'm OK," but they're not. The doorman needs to spot the trouble-makers, the pukers, and move them on before they spoil the evening. I'd be letting down the club or party hosts if I let in every nutter. Again, this comes down to experience.

It's always necessary to ensure there are enough bouncers on the door to keep trouble under lock and key. If I'm having to collect invites, show people inside and also keep an eye on customers on the pavement, things are going to get out of hand. I don't usually work anywhere – not even a gentle music-industry bash – without at least one other guy to cover my back.

Like minders, I've found that the best door hosts aren't iron-swingers straight out of the local gym. The bouncer is supposed to monitor the crowd and respond to any situation that arises. That doesn't just mean wiping their knuckles over someone's teeth. So the best guys will be capable of forming more meaningful relationships than with a dumbbell. They're going to need to be able to talk to people, to have a conversation without coming over like a threat on legs. The best bouncers don't hit first. They think first.

A well-trained bouncer will also remind people that they have a certain obligation, too. Many people don't go out with the intention of causing offence, but having me or someone like me around reminds them that they can't get away with slamming back a dozen zombies and then thumping the nearest bloke.

A night club is all about somewhere to have a good time, somewhere to relax. The best bouncer is going to be able to manage the guests inside and ensure no one gets too aggressive. It's amazing how quickly a sweet-natured kid can turn into a raging monkey after a few port and brandies. I always watch for changes in behaviour. That's part of the job, to check that no one starts to get out of hand. If they do, have a quiet word. Nothing too hard, just a gentle reminder: "Look, son, you're acting like a prat in front of your girl. Settle down, or it could get embarrassing." I can often just use body language or a bit of eye contact to let someone know I'm watching them.

A lot of places I've been asked to work aren't your down-dirty Saturday-night puke joints. I'm doing charity events, premières, high-class parties. Now, Brad Pitt isn't going to run riot, but some C-list celeb could get a little out of hand, maybe trying to get some column inches the next day, tries to pull a stunt which is neither funny nor clever. Maybe there's a bit of filthy language going about. This is where it's always good to know who people are. Take time out to read the celeb magazines. *Hello! OK!* They're all good for business. Also check the diary pages of newspapers. Watch out for the new TV and film stars. No one wants to see Johnny Depp thrown out the joint.

If the situation develops downwards – the customer starts mouthing off – then this is when the bouncer needs to have a discreet word. Hopefully, this is going to put the lid on it, calm them down. If a second reminder is necessary, make sure the irritant knows what's happening: "One more fuck-up from you and you're out, mate." Everyone knows where they stand now. Always give them the warning. Three strikes and you're out. Doesn't matter what it is. Bad language, bad behaviour, bad shit – it makes no odds. They're out.

The biggest mistake a doorman can make is to ignore someone or something that is getting out of hand. That will just escalate. Get in early to calm things. Take the heat out of the situation. That is the best policy for avoiding fights. That's the worst-case scenario, having a scrap on your hands.

But sometimes fights are inevitable. Some blokes and women are always looking for trouble. Doesn't matter where they're going. They'd have a fight with a vicar in his church, if they could. Others get aggressive with a few bottles of booze inside them. Maybe they meet up with someone they've already got a beef with inside the club. The doorman isn't going to be aware of every simmering row that's going on, but he's got to watch for it, be aware of rival gangs. If he spots trouble, out the door, straight away. Without prejudice.

Now, no one likes to be thrown out of a place they've paid to get into. I wouldn't like it. Worse still if they've been invited to a party and are asked to leave. There's no reason anyone should get boosted, but being invited somewhere doesn't give people the right to act like jerks. The best way of handling a situation where you've got to eject someone is to separate the offender from his mates or gang. Have a word or two. "I warned you. Now you're out, pal." This isn't going to be easy – timing will play a part – but it's likely to reduce the likelihood of an aggressive exchange. I can guarantee that a doorman approaching a bunch of lads and asking one to leave will only result in a barrage of four-letter words.

For safety, the Weaver rule of thumb for removing someone from a club or party is always to have at least one more person around than the number of unruly customers you are ejecting. If a larger group – of four, five or more punters – is going to be ejected, then at least double the number of bouncers that may be necessary.

Another rule is that a good bouncer should never use physical force. Not unless he has been attacked. Self-defence is OK. Obviously, I've had to protect myself on a few occasions, but I've never gone in swinging first. That's the best way to end up in the dock on a grievous bodily assault charge. Also, neck locks, arm locks or anything else which could cause injury should be avoided. Now, this doesn't mean you can't put a guiding arm around a customer. Just steer him to the door and explain why he's being put outside. Keep it calm. Don't get aggressive.

Alf and the team

Alf at the offices of M&A Security, 1990s

I can't pretend you're not going to get some verbals standing in front of a club door, barring entry, so always expect some close-to-the-knuckle language. That's always better than a real knuckle in the chops. Blokes brawling are bad for business, and the decent, money-spending crowd won't come around again if a club or bar is drawing a violent element.

Of course, not everyone is quite as firm as me, and there are always going to be ways to get past the velvets. Everyone has a story about how they blagged their way into Madonna's VIP party. I don't believe half of them, but it isn't impossible to get beyond the velvet ropes. It just needs a bit of guile. Use some street smarts. And don't start messing with the red rope. That's the best way to end up on the pavement all night.

The first message for anyone wanting to get into a place is to be original. I've heard every story there is. Twice. "Oh, please let me in. My sister is in there. She's going to have a fit and I've got her medicine." Sad story, but unbelievable. "I've lost my house keys." Nope. That won't work, either. "Please, Mr Bouncer. I'm a friend of the DJ's." Yeah, and so is the rest of the queue back there. No way, José. I'll always give tales like this the elbow.

Don't say you're a friend of the owner, either. Unless you are, or at least you know what his name is. A good friend of the owner or party-giver isn't going to be standing in line.

But if you think I'm going to give you the magical lines to swan past my colleagues, think again. Use your own imagination. Definitely don't reach for the old classic line, "Don't you know who I am?" I couldn't even guess how many times people have tried this on me. And do you know what? I never have known who they were. If they were worth knowing, I'd know them. Guys like me get paid to know who's who.

So what works? Nothing much, if it's me you're dealing with. But I've seen a few tricks in the trade work. The most effective is bribery. Now, if I see this happening with one of my guys, they're out. We're paid to only let people in who are supposed to be there, not those who can buy their way into a club or party. However, a discreetly slipped 20-spot can work dividends. It's obviously going to help if you're a blonde with all the kit. A skinny-ass geezer with bad personal hygiene is a low-priority admittance.

A word about clothes. Now, I may be biased, but I like well turned out. Nice suit and all that. But failing that, smart is going to get the nod over grunge, unless your name is Pitt or Depp. So no trainers. It doesn't matter if they're Hermes or Prada or Stan Smith. The club is playing music to dance to, not for an aerobics session. Save the trainers for Sunday afternoons at the gym. So, girls in heels – yep. But not white, OK? Boys in nice leather shoes. Black is good. Cowboy boots are only acceptable if I'm working a gay bar.

The other thing about fellas is that they turn up in pairs, threesomes, sometimes a fourball. This is a bad mistake. If men want to get inside a party, they need to bring a girl, preferably some hot young chick. Parties or clubs always work better with a higher quota of birds to blokes, and a good bouncer is always going to have some rough numbers in his head. He sees a gang of guys, he's going to refuse them entry to keep his tits-and-ass levels right. Then he'll point them to the nearest gay bar.

The best tip is always to treat the bouncer nice. Doormen are seen as the scum of the Earth by a lot of folks. I'm going to remember the little runt who called me an asshole for most of last Friday evening. He's not getting past the ropes. Ever. Maybe you've got a problem with bouncers. You don't like them. But they're only human. You treat them well, chances are they'll treat you well. It's simple. It's never hurt someone's chances of moving past me quicker if they've give me a nice pearly-white smile and then thanked me after a evening inside, even given me a tip. "Thanks, Alf, for a lovely evening." I might put that face in the old memory box and, next time they're around, cut down the waiting time.

Calling ahead to a club is also a good trick. I did this when I was driving some of the old Stax stars. Ask for the manager and say you're coming over with an important client who is something in the club, music or PR game. Be nice. It might work. They might put you on the list.

Failing all this, I've come up with the three Weaver Ps. They might not get you into a party, but remember them and at least you won't immediately be blackballed at the door. Don't get pissed, don't get prissy and don't get punchy. With these in the back pocket, you're halfway there. Otherwise, buy your own club. And put me on the velvets.

12 *Giving Up The Fags*

I had pretty well wrapped things up by the time the millennium came around, called it a day after 35 years. It was about time. I'd already handed Jerry Judge the reins at M&A and he was doing a good job. Status Quo couldn't tour forever, and nor could I.

Another reason I knocked the minding game on the head was that I'd met a beautiful new woman, Ella. We were both looking for someone else. Our careers were over and we'd both got a marriage behind us, had kids, the usual stuff. We hit it off. We both like dogs. That counts. It was time to hang up my cummerbund, put the bow tie in mothballs.

I sold up the flat in Ellerton Road and Ella put her gaff on the market and we moved down to a beautiful little village in Kent. West Malling. Right down there, right down by the railway line. Just like in Camden Town. Sit in the garden and the trains crash by on their way to France. It doesn't look like I'll ever escape those trains.

There's no rising at dawn, now, heading off on the tour bus, destination: far-flung town, off for weeks with the next new band on the block. No late nights on the door at another hip fashion party, checking the guest list. In fact, no more late nights at all. Not unless I want them. The days are filled with Arsenal – I've still got my season ticket; I watch every home match – and holidays. It's like an extended vacation. We like cruises at Christmas. That keeps us out of trouble. We've done a few big sails, recently. One around the Far East – Singapore, Vietnam (north and south), Bali and the Philippines – another in the Caribbean and one around Central America, through the Panama Canal. I'm never short of a dinner jacket when we're called up to the captain's table.

I'm also trying to give up the fags. You've got to look after your health, haven't you? Ella has got me on the nicotine patches, but I'm still popping outside for a quick puff. Frank was never successful at kicking, but I hope I can.

I'm also putting in the hours on my golf swing. There's a couple of good courses around Kent. That's where I can brush up my short game. Well, what else is retirement for? The handicap isn't coming down, but it does give me time to reflect on life. And often I slip back to thinking about the industry I helped spawn, the bodyguard business. More specifically, the rock 'n' roll bodyguard business.

The bodyguard has now become part of the media game, an extension of a star's ego. Another bauble to collect, like the limo and the loaned Julien Macdonald dress for the red-carpet walk. That's not what I got in the game for, but that's life, as they say. I remember when *The Bodyguard* came out, the film with Kevin Costner. Gary Kemp playing Whitney Houston's manager. He did a good job there. I did a load of TV and radio around that. Everyone wanted to talk to me, because I was the prototype. What they wanted to know was, what sort of legacy have I left? It's something I now ask myself, usually around the ninth hole.

To tell the truth, sometimes I wonder if I've played a hand in creating a monster. The minder monster. I cringe when I see pop stars ride into town nowadays with more bodyguards than underpants. I've done security for Prince, in the past. There would be times when he'd have us. Then he'd bring in another four of his own massive goons to follow him around. What's that about? Just feeding the ego, because a bodyguard should only be seen if there's a problem. This was one-upmanship. "I've got more bodyguards than you." Some other celebrity hits town with eight minders. "Hey, I've got more than you now, Prince." Someone else gets in. "Yeah, but mine are bigger than yours." It's like kids in the playground.

I also used to wonder why some people needed minders in the first place. Sure, Kylie Minogue may get bothered by a few kids, but her sister, Dannii? Nah. Often, it seems the lower down the celebrity league people are, the more minders they think are necessary. I've seen A-list stars arrive at parties on their tod. Then some no-mark I'd be hard-pressed to recognise turns up with a bunch of bruisers in tow. Who are they kidding? It's not like anyone would have mobbed them if they'd walked down the road naked. But I guess, if they're paying the bills at the end of the night, what's the harm?

Another thing that worries me is the unwarranted aggression that some new-style minders employ. That's ugly. Don't get me wrong, a bodyguard has sometimes got to be confrontational – it's part of the job description to get tough and kick ass – but that doesn't mean I'm going to act like a bull

24 hours a day. There's no need to get hot under the collar. Unless someone is giving me bother.

But I've seen this new breed of aggressive minder grow. They're always at boiling point, ready to go steaming in. And they do. Often they can be too rough on fans, which is defeating the whole object of a good night out. No singer or group wants their fans roughed up. A bad-ass attitude from a bodyguard will also end up creating its own trouble. Aggression feeds aggression. Trouble that could probably have been snuffed out with the odd word or two can, with a hard-nosed minder, end up with two guys brawling it out. These guys are giving us a bad press. They're not good for the profession. That's a shame, because it devalues the whole minding business.

And it's a serious business. Sometimes it can also be a dangerous one. Not 99 per cent of the time, but it only takes a moment of madness for someone to get hurt. Ask Yoko Ono. What happened to John Lennon was tragic. His killing turned every rock and film star's life around. Before that, the worst pop stars expected was a mauling, getting mobbed, a nasty letter now and again. But catching a bullet, that's a different thing. Scary. I don't know why John hadn't got someone with him that night, but he'd probably be alive today if he had. I wish I'd been there.

That's the job of the minder, to be around and to stop any trouble. And this is why I'm proud to have called myself a minder. I know I've stopped a lot of trouble, prevented a lot of people from getting hurt. And it's why the rock 'n' roll bodyguard has become an essential part of the celebrity's kit. Part of the fabric. They're necessary.

I've also managed to enjoy myself along the way. I really can't think of a better way to have spent my life, going around the world with rock stars and getting paid for it. If I was killed now, I'd die happy. What's really extraordinary is that I never had a plan. No Weaver strategic plan. That's what the corporate high-rollers say, isn't it? Certainly not when I was on the knocker. Knocking those houses in York, I had no idea that I'd eventually be running one of Britain's leading security companies. I'm just grateful that I got there in the end, that it happened for me.

Being a bodyguard also meant I got to meet a whole bunch of people from all walks of life, from the celebs down to the guys on the door at their record companies. As I said, some were fantastic. Some weren't. I've also got some terrific memories of working with the greats. No one can take those away. They're in the bank. Funny little moments, like with Robbie

Alf with his dogs on Wandsworth Common, January 1992, wearing the same coat and boots bought for him by Mike Nesmith for the Alaskan trip

Williams. No fists flying, just him and me hanging at my house. The pair of us sitting on my grotty back-room sofa cheering on his team, Port Vale, in a cup game, cracking a few beers. Rob's got a big voice. I can vouch for that. Port Vale scored and Rob went mad, jumping up and down. Scared the dogs. Christ, he scared me. Almost.

Index